Corrections
in
America

LAW AND CRIMINAL JUSTICE SERIES

Series Editor: James A. Inciardi
Division of Criminal Justice, University of Delaware

The **Law and Criminal Justice Series** provides students in criminal justice, criminology, law, sociology, and related fields with a set of short textbooks on major topics and subareas of the field. The texts range from books that introduce the basic elements of criminal justice for lower-division undergraduates to more advanced topics of current interest for advanced undergraduates and beginning graduate students. Each text is concise, didactic, and produced in an inexpensive paperback as well as hardcover format. Each author addresses the major issues and areas of current concern in that topic area, reporting on and synthesizing major research done on the subject. Case examples, chapter summaries, and discussion questions are generally included in each volume to aid in classroom use. The modular format of the series provides attractive alternatives to large, expensive classroom textbooks and timely supplements to more traditional class materials.

Volumes in this series:

Additional volumes currently in development.

Corrections in America

Problems of the Past and the Present

CHARLES W. THOMAS

Volume 7.
Law and Criminal Justice Series

SAGE PUBLICATIONS
The Publishers of Professional Social Science
Newbury Park   Beverly Hills   London   New Delhi

TO LEWIS AND JEANNE DIANA

For information address:

SAGE Publications, Inc.
2111 West Hillcrest Drive
Newbury Park, California 91320

SAGE Publications Inc. SAGE Publications Ltd.
275 South Beverly Drive   28 Banner Street
Beverly Hills   London EC1Y 8QE
California 90212   England

SAGE PUBLICATIONS India Pvt. Ltd.
M-32 Market
Greater Kailash I
New Delhi 110 048 India

Printed in the United States of America

Library of Congress Cataloging-in-Publication Data

Main entry under title:

Thomas, Charles Wellington, 1943-
    Corrections in America.

    (Law and criminal justice series ; v. 7)
    Includes bibliographies and index.
    1. Corrections—United States.   2. Criminal justice,
Administration of—United States.   3. Crime and
criminals—United States.   4. Punishment—United States.
I. Title.   II. Series.
HV9471.T47   1986   364.6'0973   85-27872
ISBN 0-8039-2210-8
ISBN 0-8039-2211-6 (pbk.)

CONTENTS

PREFACE

Too often, I think, those of us working within that portion of criminology referred to as "the field of corrections" have devoted too little of our attention to the fundamental legal, moral, and scientific aspects of penology in favor of littering the criminological landscape with piles of research on more narrowly defined issues. To our collective embarrassment, many of us have come to understand that the sum total of our present knowledge base contains virtually no sound theories by means of which we can go about the business of explaining the phenomena that attract our interest and even less information on which those working within our criminal justice system can rely in their quest for practical guidelines.

Nor is the embarrassment limited to a growing awareness of how little we know. Not long ago, there were more than a few of us who applauded the infrequency with which such words as "punishment" had come to be used and who were excited by the prospect that rehabilitation might be the only goal that any legislator or trial court judge would have in mind when the provisions of criminal law were being constructed or applied. The pursuit of rehabilitative goals, it was said, was something that experts like us knew how to achieve—if, of course, we were given enough time, financial support, and, of course, power. Now we can look back on at least a century of experience, billions of dollars of expenditures, and the consequences of our having exercised a good deal of power. What we see is failure. What we see is still another illustration of how good intentions can pave the road to hell. The body of criminal law on which we rely is a maze of conflicts, contradictions, and, too often, an expression of special rather than general interests. The system by means of which that body of law is applied works in a haphazard fashion at best and in a discriminatory fashion more often than most realize. Our efforts to deal with the hundreds of thousands of offenders who appear annually before our criminal courts is nothing short of a national disgrace.

In short, those who study penology have little reason to be happy. They have come to learn that they have numerous questions about how and why and with what effects punishment is imposed on those convicted by our courts but that the number of answers they can provide for those questions is quite small. Indeed, it is a frustrating position in which we now find ourselves. If the imagination needs more fuel before it can appreciate that frustration, the chapters that follow should serve that need quite well.

My purpose has not been to provide a comprehensive textbook on the field of penology (or the field of corrections). Instead, I have sought to identify and discuss some of what I take to be the most basic kinds of issues and problems that confront the people—both academics and practitioners—working in the field today. Both by choice and as a consequence of the small size of the volumes in the Sage Foundations of Criminal Justice Series, focusing on these general issues and problems presents significant limitations for some readers. Such specific and important concerns as women in prison, community-based correctional strategies, the special problems presented by

juvenile or youthful offenders, probation, and parole receive little or no detailed attention. In their place one finds more thorough attentiveness to such general concerns as
the history of penology, how we go about the difficult task of justifying the use of
punishment, the heated debate that now rages between those who favor and those who
oppose the traditional rehabilitative model, our uses and abuses of imprisonment as a
means of achieving a broad array of often conflicting goals, and our continued willingness to rely on capital punishment. My only academic excuse for granting much attention to some general topics and little or none to more specific issues is that I am convinced that the needs of beginning students of penology are best served by their first
coming to grips with the broad differences of opinion that are changing this field of inquiry and practice so dramatically. Should their interest in the field remain strong, they
can then seek out alternative sources for information on more specialized topics.

ACKNOWLEDGMENTS

I have learned that writing any book—even a small one like this—puts authors in an impossible position. Perhaps it would be more accurate to say that it puts everyone who has to deal with authors in an impossible position. My wife and children, for instance, have recently come to wonder if I remember their names. I have certainly exhausted the tolerance of my colleagues after asking them to read and reread versions of one or more of the following chapters. I suspect that my students would like to become something other than the objects of lectures that are too often limited to whatever topic I happened to have been writing about the day before they walked into one of my classes.

Having freely admitted to these and related sins of omission and commission, I can do little more than acknowledge a few of those on whom I have depended either directly or indirectly in approaching the work on this volume. Certainly one of those persons is Hugo Adam Bedau of Tufts University's Department of Philosophy. Much of what appears here is a consequence of his long-standing contention that criminologists should no longer tolerate their own ignorance of the world of philosophy. Though he will quickly see that the ignorance he detected many years ago has not disappeared, I hope that he will appreciate the efforts that have been made to follow his always sound advice.

I must also acknowledge the role played by my friends and criminological colleagues at the University of Florida: Ron Akers, Donna Bishop, Alexis Durham, Chuck Frazier, Dick Hollinger, Lonn Lanza-Kaduce, Mike Radelet, Pam Richards, and Fred Shenkman. There quite simply is no more productive nor more congenial a group of criminologists at any other single university in the nation. While each of them will join with Hugo Bedau in noting many features of what follows that could and should have been handled better than I was able to handle them, those problems would have been all the more obvious had it not been for what they have taught me during the five years that I have been at the University of Florida.

Finally, it is with much affection and respect that I dedicate this book to Lewis and Jeanne Diana. They entered the academic world after completing their doctoral degrees in sociology at the University of Pittsburgh while I was trying to survive the rigors of elementary school. In their initial capacities as aunt and uncle, and later in their roles as valued colleagues when I joined the faculty of Virginia Commonwealth University, they provided a set of personal and professional standards that can only be described as exemplary. I hope that both will detect something of their considerable influence in portions of what follows.

—*Charles W. Thomas*

1

THE STUDY OF PENOLOGY

In 1964 William James Rummel was convicted by a Texas court for the felony offense of using a credit card with the intent to defraud another of roughly $80.00. He was sentenced to a term of three years of confinement. In 1969 Rummel was convicted of a second felony offense after he passed a forged check in the amount of $28.36. He was sentenced to a term of four years of imprisonment. In 1973 he was convicted of a third felony after he accepted $120.75 with the promise of repairing an air conditioner that he never actually repaired. The applicable Texas statute for this offense provides for confinement in a penitentiary for a term of not less than two nor more than ten years. However, Texas law contains a separate statute under which Rummel could be prosecuted. That statute permits but does not require Texas prosecutors to contend that offenders who (1) have been convicted of two previous felonies (2) for which they have been sentenced to a term of imprisonment and (3) who are subsequently charged with a third felony offense are habitual offenders.

Although Texas law defines the status of being a habitual offender as an entirely separate criminal offense, in this instance the burden on the prosecution to prove its case was obviously minimal. It would simply have to prove that Rummel did commit the felony offense of fraudulently taking the $120.75 for work that he never performed, produce evidence that he had been convicted of two previous felonies, and show that each of those two prior felony convictions had resulted in a sentence of imprisonment. Conviction on a charge of being a habitual offender carries with it a mandatory sentence of life imprisonment.

Having established what Texas prosecutors *could* have done, what in fact *should* they have done? Should they have looked at the nature of Rummel's third offense and satisfied themselves with the possibility that he would confront a term of from two to ten years of confinement? Should they have been troubled by the possibility of a two-to-ten-year sentence for an offense that involved nothing more than the fraudulent taking of only $120.75? How much importance should they have attached to the fact that Rummel had been convicted and served prison time on two previous occasions? Had he "paid his debt to society" by serving those earlier sentences, or should his third felony offense have been thought of as especially serious simply because it was a third offense? Is part of your feeling about how this case should have been handled influenced by the hypothesis that he is the kind of offender who seems likely to commit more offenses in the future. If so, how comfortable do you feel when you understand that defining his third offense as especially serious because you believe there is a high probability of future criminality puts you in the potentially awkward position of recommending a harsher punishment today for offenses that have not yet been—and indeed might not ever be—committed? In other words, should we punish people for what they have done, or for what we think they might do in the future?

Regardless of whether or not you feel that Rummel's record of two prior felony offenses should influence the definition and disposition of his third offense, what reasonable goal might we seek to achieve by the sentence imposed? How harsh or lenient a sentence seems appropriate in light of the goal or goals you have in mind? Moreover, how would you go about determining the extent to which the goals you favor have been achieved? What would you recommend were we to find that your recommended case disposition failed to achieve the objectives you had in mind? For example, would you react to such evidence by making your recommended punishment harsher or more lenient when you encountered similar cases in the future?

These, of course, are tediously difficult questions. In large measure they are questions for which we have few if any answers. Nevertheless, Mr. Rummel's record is in many ways typical of what we find in the records of tens of thousands of people who appear before our criminal courts each and every year. His crimes were relatively trivial; the sum total of his three theft offenses gained him a less-than-awesome $229.11. There is no indication of his having been armed at the time of any of his offenses. There is no indication that he ever used or threatened to use force or violence in the furtherance of any of his criminal plans, nor that the seriousness or harmfulness of his criminal behavior was escalating. At the same time, however, Rummel had served time in a Texas penitentiary after his 1964 conviction. Some years after his release, he committed another crime, served additional prison time, and committed still another crime. The State of Texas appears to have been unsuccessful in its efforts either to rehabilitate or deter him. The state was obviously having a good deal of trouble with an offender who, while never involved in offenses that most of us would view as especially serious, had made a habit of crime despite repeated efforts to persuade him to avoid such contact. Should the Texas prosecutor, in effect, have given up on Rummel by charging him with being a habitual offender and thereby seeking the mandatory sentence of life imprisonment? If not, how often should Texas prosecutors have looked at each new offense as though his prior record were irrelevant?

Suffice it to say that the State of Texas determined that Mr. Rummel was a sufficient threat to its citizens that he deserved to be charged with both a third felony offense and a violation of its habitual offender statute. Consistent with the provisions of the applicable Texas law, the trial court sentenced Rummel to the mandatory term of life imprisonment in a Texas penitentiary. He challenged the constitutionality of his sentence by contending that a mandatory term of life imprisonment for such a modest record of unlawful conduct was prohibited by the provision of the Eighth Amendment to the Constitution which prohibits the imposition of cruel and unusual punishment. Eventually this challenge came before the Supreme Court of the United States (*Rummel v. Estelle,* 445 U.S. 263, 1980). Partly because Texas law included the possibility—though certainly not a guarantee—that Rummel might eventually be released on parole, the Supreme Court held that the sentence imposed on him was not consitutionally defective. His sentence of life imprisonment remained in place.

We need not deal further with *Rummel v. Estelle* or related cases in this chapter. I describe it here as a concrete illustration of the subject matter of this slim volume. This is a book about our reactions to those who have been found guilty of violating the provisions of criminal law. It is a book about the forms of punishment on which we have come to depend most commonly, about the justifications we advance when we are called upon to explain why we permit the state to impose these types of punishment, and about how well or poorly punishment serves the goals for which it is intended. It is a book about the paradox we create when, on the one hand, we claim to be the citizens of an advanced and civilized society and yet, on the other hand, find no flaw in supporting punishments that are psychologically and physically brutal. It is also a book about the substantial efforts we have made to insulate those whose offensive and harmful behavior has resulted in their being convicted from the still harsher plight they could confront were the rule of law not available to protect them against the victims of crimes who cry out for vengeance rather than justice. It is a book about the most important of a small number of contexts within which the state claims the right to deprive its citizens of their liberty, and the only context within which the state claims the right to deprive them of their lives. It is also a book about how the state goes to great lengths to protect the rights of those citizens whose predatory behavior reflects their disregard for the rights of their fellow citizens.

The territory that we need to cover is large. The issues are often complex. Our ability to deal with these issues in a suitably objective manner will often have been undermined by the biases we have adopted even before we begin. Most readers, for example, could easily express some firm opinions about the questions I have posed regarding how the *Rummel* case should have been handled even if they had never studied crime in anything akin to traditional academic courses. Crime and punishment, after all, are hardly areas of inquiry about which readers have no existing opinions and in which they have no experience. To the contrary, it is most unlikely that any of us can survive a day without being bombarded with information about crime and legal reactions (not to mention illegal reactions) to it. To cite the most obvious example, the mass media have long recognized our fear of and fascination with crime. The media make a handsome profit from exploiting this fear and fascination through what is rightly or wrongly said to constitute news and through an endless set of even less factual variations on the "cops and robbers" theme. The effects of this exposure to the world of crime and punishment are so obvious and so pervasive that no list of examples seems necessary. Indeed, the fact that my six-year-old son just reacted to my telling him to clean up his room by pointing a toy pistol at me and inviting me to "make his day" convinces me that these effects begin to manifest themselves long before adulthood.

Of no less importance is the likelihood that readers will have had vicarious and perhaps personal experience in one or more of the areas we encounter here. The evidence strongly suggests that many if not most of us have or will have experience *both* as offenders *and* as victims. A small library full of criminological research, for example, suggests that the vast majority of us have committed one or more criminal acts which, if they had been detected and prosecuted, could have resulted in our being labeled as criminal (e.g., Nettler, 1984: 81-97). The likelihood of our being the victims of crime is also high. Even if we were to limit our attention to crimes committed against private citizens (as opposed to also considering crimes committed against businesses, the government, public property, and so on), we would have to anticipate some 40 million criminal victimizations this year alone (Bureau of Justice Statistics, 1984b). This means that nearly one-third of all the households in the nation will have been touched by some crime of violence or theft before the end of the year (Bureau of Justice Statistics, 1984a).

Difficult or not, we must begin to organize the materials that deserve consideration in some systematic way. A preliminary step in this direction is taken in this chapter, which has three purposes. First, some passing attention has to be given to what the study of punishment is all about and how it can best be categorized in terms of the various academic disciplines devoted to the study of human behavior. Second, given the high probability that those reading this book are not and do not aspire to become specialists in this particular area of inquiry, some consideration of why punishment deserves to be studied by nonspecialists seems necessary. Finally, so that the reader will have some ability to anticipate where this discussion is going and why, the chapter concludes with a brief description of how the remaining portions of the book are organized.

WHAT IS "CORRECTIONS"?

Identifying the specialized area of academic study within which the topics addressed in this volume find the greatest emphasis is not as easy as you might think. Representatives of several behavioral science disciplines—especially criminology, psychology, and sociology—have claimed that the study of punishment most properly falls within the territorial limits of their chosen discipline. Because the focus of the bulk of the research has been on various facets of punishment and its consequences, and also because of the placement of academic courses dealing with these issues, the discipline of sociology was more or less acknowledged as the "parent discipline" until a decade or two ago. Even today there are many who think of the study of punishment as an area of inquiry that falls primarily within the scope of that subfield of sociology which is referred to as the *sociology of corrections*. This area of sociology involves the study of social and legal reactions to those who have been convicted of crimes and how such reactions shape their future lives and life chances. The sociology of corrections is thus closely related in many ways to other subfields of sociology within which sociologists study our reactions to types of behavior that, while defined as undesirable or inappropriate, are not defined as violations of criminal law (i.e., the *sociology of deviance*).

The traditional view that the study of punishment and its consequences falls within the discipline of sociology can, I think, no longer be thought of as being reasonable or acceptable by anyone other than a handful of sociologists who have an amusingly imperial view of the scope of their discipline. Instead, it seems clear that the materials reviewed in this book fall within a subfield of the discipline of *criminology* that is called *penology*. Criminology is an academic discipline that is devoted to (1) furthering our understanding of the processes by means of which criminal law is created, modified, and applied and (2) creating explanations for both why criminal law is violated and why we react to violations of law in the ways that we do. Penology can be defined roughly as that portion of criminology which is devoted to the study of punishment and its consequences. Given the concerns of criminology in general and penology in particular, it is only natural that there be an "applied" branch of each. *Criminal justice* is perhaps the most widely used term for the application-oriented aspects of criminology. Corrections is the (inacurrate, I think) term that is used most commonly by those working in such areas of "applied penology" as probation, prison-based programs, and parole.

Criminologists and criminal justice practitioners whose major interests are in some aspect of penology thus involve themselves in the study or actual application of punishment. However, it is important to understand that the scope of penology is far broader than what may be implied by so matter-of-fact a phrase as "the study of punishment." Penology includes, to choose but a few of the more obvious and important illustrations, a serious concern with the evolution of punishment (i.e., its history), how we go about the difficult but very important task of defining the circumstances under which the state has the right to create law and then impose punishment on those citizens found guilty of unlawful conduct (i.e., moral philosophy), the body of law that defines what the state may do and must refrain from doing in its reactions to offenders (i.e., constitutional and correctional law), the design and operation of programs intended to modify one or more characteristics of offenders (and here penologists draw on and contribute to the developments of such fields as education, psychology, psychiatry, medicine, and sociology), and scientific assessments of how our various reactions to offenders influence their future attitudes, values, behavior, and life chances (i.e., evaluation research). Thus, notwithstanding the continuing frequency with which penology and the sociology of corrections are used as though the two areas of inquiry were one and the same, the practice seems altogether falacious. Much, if not most, of what attracts the attention of penologists is far removed from what attracts the attention of sociologists. Furthermore, it seems fairly obvious that the use of the term "corrections" either by sociologists or by those working in areas like probation, prisons, and parole is deceptive. The fact that much of what motivates social and legal reactions to offenders often has little or nothing to do with "correcting" them has been well established.

What's in a Name?

It may seem trivial to bother with a discussion of whether the subject matter of a book like this one falls within the disciplinary boundaries of criminology versus such related disciplines as anthropology, political science, psychology, or sociology. If that is your feeling, then I suspect you are correct in feeling that way. My concern for the categorization of the kind of work that I do may stem largely from the frustration I feel when other academics refer to me as a sociologist when I am convinced that I am a criminologist. The frustration has only increased since I moved to the University of Florida some years ago and became a criminology professor. The University of Florida has been so slow in keeping up with the changes in the academic world that its administration is not yet convinced that criminology is a fully legitimate area of study. Worse yet, there is a feeling that anyone involved in criminology is primarily involved with the business of writing traffic tickets, emptying parking meters, and "lifting" fingerprints from ice cubes.

Moving to the South and trying to remain in the 20th century are not always goals that can be easily achieved at the same time. Fortunately, those with serious interests in studying criminology at either the undergraduate or graduate level have more excellent options available to them today than at any other point in the history of the discipline. Depending largely on the particular aspect of criminology in which they are especially concerned, that list of choices would certainly include Arizona State University, Florida State University, the University of Maryland, Michigan State University, the University of Pennsylvania, Pennsylvania State University, Rutgers University, and the State University of New York at Albany (see, e.g., Thomas and Bronick, 1984).

The business of naming a field of inquiry can be much more than an illustration of the fondness that academicians have for splitting semantic hairs. Regardless of whether one thinks of the study of the goals and consequences of punishment as falling within the territorial limits of one versus another academic discipline or as an interdisciplinary affair, one must have serious reservations about the wisdom of naming the area of inquiry "corrections." I think that doing so suggests that the primary objective of our reactions to offenders is to correct them—to change them in some way from something that we define as unacceptable into something that we feel is more appropriate. Over the past two or three decades it has certainly become fashionable to refrain from using terms like "penology" and instead to adopt terms like "corrections." The study of penology thus came to be referred to as the study of corrections, prisons came to be referred to as correctional institutions, and prison guards came to be referred to as correctional officers.

During the same time period, however, little if anything really changed on anything other than a purely semantic level. The same kinds of people appear today before the same kinds of courts. They receive much the same kinds of sentences. They are committed to the same kinds of institutions. They encounter the same kinds of treatment at the hands of the same kinds of people. Their rates of recidivism (i.e., the likelihood of new offenses after release from "correctional supervision") have remained substantially the same. Not much, in short, has changed in the world of punishment and its consequences—other than another demonstration of our fondness for euphemisms, our attraction to substituting positively valued expressions (e.g., "the field of corrections") for negatively valued expressions (e.g., "punishment").

What such euphemisms can do is make us feel better about what we do without any need to change what is actually done. For example, it might seem harsh and punitive were we to commit an offender to a term of five to ten years at hard labor in a state penitentiary after his or her conviction for some modest criminal offense. It somehow seems to be almost an act of grace and benevolence, however, when we do precisely the same thing in precisely the same place under the supervision of precisely the same people but describe it as commitment to a State Department of Corrections with a requirement for meaningful involvement in appropriate rehabilitative and vocational educational programs. At least it seems better to those who do not have to do the time. In my many years of prison research, I have yet to see an inmate who felt better because we called the place within which he or she was confined a correctional institution rather than a penitentiary, because those supervising him or her were known as correctional officers rather than prison guards, or because the monotony of stamping out license plates was defined as vocational training rather than hard labor.

My point, then, is quite simple. Naming that which we are about to consider "the study of corrections" or "the study of penology" presents us with a significant rather than a trivial problem. The former term is inaccurate and misleading. It is inaccurate because the bulk of what takes place within our "correctional system" has pitifully little to do with anything even remotely related to "correcting" or "rehabilitating." It is misleading because our inclination to speak in terms of corrections can and does result in our thinking of our reactions to offenders as though they were largely motivated by a desire to intervene in the lives of those offenders in a positive and therapeutic fashion. I doubt that such motives are nearly as salient as our reliance on euphemisms might suggest. I doubt, for example, that those who sentenced William Rummel to a term of life imprisonment had even a remote objective of diagnosing any problems he may have had and then involving him in such a well-conceived "correctional" program that he would thereby become a productive member of society. Despite its title, therefore, this is a book about how and why and with what effects we rely on punishment in our dealings with those convicted of crimes. A part of what we consider, to be sure, has to do with those of our efforts that are aimed at treatment, rehabilitation, and correction. However, that part, as well as other dimensions of our discussion, falls within the broader scope of penology.

WHY STUDY PENOLOGY?

It is unlikely that more than a small fraction of those who encounter this book will have chosen criminology in general or penology in particular as their primary area of academic or professional interest. Indeed, even among those who have well-developed interests in and commitments to the field of criminology, penology continues to be something of a bastard child. Most introductory criminology textbooks, for example, either deal with the subject matter of penology in little more than a sketchy fashion or ignore the area altogether (e.g., Quinney, 1979; Conklin, 1981; Barlow, 1984; Fox, 1985; Michalowski, 1985). It might be useful, therefore, to discuss an obvious question: Why bother? Why be concerned with penology unless it is of direct relevance to one's chosen area of specialization?

It seems to me that these questions have any number of reasonable answers. Perhaps the most obvious is that there are few problems of life in contemporary society that affect so many people in such adverse ways as does crime. As was indicated earlier, for example, there are ample reasons to believe that this year will witness something on the order of one out of every three households in the United States being the object of one or more of the 40 million criminal victimizations that are likely to occur this year (Bureau of Justice Statistics, 1984a, 1984b). Many of these victimizations, of course, will involve something other than a major criminal offense. This is part—and only part—of the reason that year in and year out, only about half of the victimizations of private citizens are reported to the police (e.g., Bureau of Justice Statistics, 1984b: 17-18). However, even if we were to focus our attention only on the fairly small set of serious felony offenses that are often incorporated into measures of the volume of major crimes—criminal homicide, rape, aggravated assault, robbery, burglary, grand theft, auto theft, and arson—we would have to anticipate something on the order of 14 million of these offenses being reported to law enforcement agencies this year.

Though translating of such huge numbers into a more manageable frame of reference presents many interpretive problems, the figures mean that the police receive a report of a serious crime of violence every 24 seconds and a report of a serious property crime every three seconds (e.g., U.S. Department of Justice, 1982: 5). These criminal victimizations are likely to result in roughly 11 million persons being arrested on criminal charges, with roughly one-fourth of these arrests involving persons charged with one or more of the serious felony offenses just listed and the balance involving persons charged with various other crimes (Brown et al., 1984: 415). Not counting the tens of billions of dollars in damages done to those who are victimized, dealing with the volume of crime in the United States—including the costs of policing, operating the judicial system, and maintaining the penal system—will cost us something in excess of $30 billion (e.g., Brown et al., 1984: 3). Of course, the total price tag on crime is far, far higher. Even a decade ago the cost of crime and our efforts to deal with it was estimated to be more than $125 billion per year (e.g., Conklin, 1981: 43-73).

An initial rationale for having an interest in penology, in other words, is that crime and our reactions to it have such a pervasive, direct, and often personal impact on each and every one of us. They are topics about which all of us must have some minimal level of literacy and knowledge. We have a very matter-of-fact, practical interest in crime and in the steps that the state claims to be taking on our behalf in its effort to bring the problem under control.

The fact that crime touches so many of us so often and in such undesirable ways, however, is certainly not the only reason that the topic warrants attention. To study penology—including why we feel justified in imposing punishment, why we feel that punishment is appropriate for some forms of conduct but inappropriate for other (and sometimes more harmful) behavior, how we go about the difficult business of determining the amount or type of punishment that we are willing to think of as just, and how we determine whether punishment has aided us in achieving the goals that prompted us to rely on it—also teachers us quite a lot about the nature and quality of the society in which we live. One might argue, for example, that a society within which the rights and liberties of individuals are held in high regard would hesitate to deprive any of its citizens of those rights and liberties. Should such deprivations be thought of as absolutely necessary, they would surely be limited to an absolute minimum. This was the view expressed more than two hundred years ago by Cesare Beccaria (1764/1963: 99), often described as the "father of criminology," when he argued: "In order for punishment not to be, in every instance, an act of violence of one or of many against a private citizen, it must be essentially public, prompt, necessary, the least possible under the given circumstances, proportionate to the crimes, dictated by the laws." Americans often like to claim that their society is one within which precisely such a high value is placed on individual rights and liberties.

One important purpose of studying penology is to compare such verbal claims with actual practice and to thereby distinguish between mere pretense and the realities of everyday life. Convicted offenders, after all, tend to be people who either have moved or have been pushed to the outer margins of our society. They are the objects of fear, anger, and distrust. In a very real sense they are members of a minority group who lack the social, economic, and political means to resist should members of the majority group seek to discriminate against them in ways that would be socially and legally unacceptable were we dealing with any other category of citizens. Therefore, to identify and understand the rights and protections that we grant to such people is to understand something about the minimum rights and protections that are available to the rest of us.

Unfortunately, the outcome of such comparisons can be disturbing. Too often they reveal that the correlation between our behavior and the values we claim to support is far from perfect. Reflect back on the situation confronted by William Rummel. When I have assigned *Rummel v. Estelle* in classes that I teach, my students are invariably shocked by the harshness of the sentence Rummel received relative to the nature of the offenses for which he was convicted.[1] They almost refuse to believe that the Supreme Court would conclude, as Justice Rehnquist did in delivering the opinion of the Court in *Rummel,* that "one could argue without fear of contradiction by any decision of this

Court that for crimes concededly classified and classifiable as felonies, that is, as punishable by significant terms of imprisonment in a state penitentiary, *the length of the sentence actually imposed is purely a matter of legislative prerogative"* (445 U.S. 274, 1980, emphasis added). Whether their political attitudes are conservative or liberal, they find it difficult to believe that the state, speaking through the members of the most powerful judicial body in the nation, would contend so flatly that limitations on the harshness of punishment are to be shaped so thoroughly by the political judgments of legislative bodies and so minimally through the moral judgments of private citizens.

In the tension that so clearly exists between the holding of the Supreme Court in *Rummel* and the moral judgments of ordinary citizens we find still another important reason for studying penology. Penology is not an important subject simply because the problems of crime and punishment touch so many of us so directly. It is not an important subject simply because it provides us with a vantage point from which we can measure more clearly the minimum rights and protections that we as individual citizens are willing to grant to the least powerful members of our society. Perhaps its greatest significance comes through its ability to focus our attention so sharply on the relationship between the state and its citizens. The context provided by a convicted defendant coming before a criminal court to be sentenced for his or her offense reveals this relationship as clearly if not more clearly than any that I can imagine. Crimes, very importantly, are legally defined as offenses committed against the state—the same state whose political processes define, among other things, the nature of the conduct that it has chosen to view as criminal, the manner in which defendants charged with crimes are to be handled, and the types and durations of punishment that convicted defendants can confront.

When most of us think about crimes, we think about one person harming another person in some way that is prohibited by law, and of the state as a more or less disinterested party that intervenes on behalf of the victim in an effort to see that justice is done. This image, however, is entirely incorrect. The state is (or at least pretends to be) a detached, neutral party only when the harm done falls into a broad area that is often referred to as *private law*. Private law seeks to define and regulate relationships between private citizens, groups, corporations, and so on. Illustrations of private law thus include family law, corporate law, patent law, copyright law, tort law, and contract law. When some violation of private law is alleged, one private party, called a *plaintiff,* initiates litigation against another private party, called a *defendant*. The state is expected to play the role of a neutral mediator. The supposed goal is to provide an objective, neutral arena—a *civil court*—within which a fair and impartial resolution of the dispute between the parties to the litigation can be reached.

Criminal cases fall into a category called *public law*. Thus they present us with a very different scenario from what we find in, for example, disputes involving private parties who are seeking a divorce, the settlement of an estate, compensation for harm caused by the negligence of another person, or payment for damages caused by the failure of another person to do what his or her contract required. In this area of public law, we find that the state has defined that some types of behavior are required (e.g., filing income tax returns) and that some types of behavior are prohibited (e.g., fraud, criminal homicide, and the like). The state also has chosen to avoid defining many other equally or even more harmful acts as crimes. It—and not the individual we might commonly think of as being the victim of a criminal offense—determines who will or will not be prosecuted. Indeed, time and time again the appellate courts have held that the specific persons who may have been the objects of criminal victimizations have no special right either to require that the offender be prosecuted or to demand that criminal charges *not* be filed (e.g., *Linda R. S. v. Richard D.*, 410 U.S. 614, 1973). The legal victim of a criminal act, you see, is the state itself.

The ability of the study of penology to reveal something important about the relationship between the state and its citizens is clearly one of the most critical contributions that studying penology can make to the education of any of us. It is a theme that will appear and reappear at many points in what is to follow, and it will often become clear that the truely awesome power of the state plays a complex—and sometimes confusing—role. On the one hand, for example, it is easy to find illustrations of how the state extends and applies its power in ways that seem excessively harsh or discriminatory and that seem designed to benefit the interests of the few at the expense of the many. The holding of the Supreme Court in *Rummel*, for example, strikes me as one that permitted an unjustifiably brutal punishment when we consider the harm done by Mr. Rummel and when we compare the magnitude of the sentence he received with the relatively trivial sentences that are routinely imposed on far more serious offenders. I am no less offended when the state either refuses to file criminal charges against or ignores altogether the obviously harmful conduct of major corporations whose executives willfully and knowingly manufacture and then sell products that are later found to be dangerous and defective. (The fairly recent case of the Ford Motor Company's liability for the sale of cars that were alleged to have dangerous defects in the design of their gasoline tanks is perhaps the best known illustration of this point; *State of Indiana v. Ford Motor Company,* 24 CrL 2454, 1979.)

On the other hand, the exercise of power by the state also serves as something of a buffer between us and those we feel have harmed us or our interests. The state can be and often is an entity that protects the interests of the few against the will of the many. Few examples would make the point any clearer than the situation we presently confront with regard to the use of capital punishment. Although the U.S. Supreme Court held that this extreme penalty was unconstitutional in 1972 (*Furman v. Georgia*, 408 U.S. 238), it adjusted its position in 1976 by holding that some types of post-*Furman* death penalty statutes were constitutionally sound (e.g., *Gregg v. Georgia*, 428 U.S. 153). Today there are roughly 1700 persons in the United States who are awaiting execution. The number actually executed since 1976 is likely to have reached more than 60 by the time this book is published.

More important for the point I wish to make here, a large number of surveys of public opinion clearly indicate that a significant majority—perhaps as many as three-quarters—of adult citizens in the United States favor capital punishment. Notwithstanding the favorable assessments of capital punishment statutes on legal grounds and the obviously high levels of public support for using so harsh a legal sanction, the state—partly through the body of criminal law and the rules of criminal procedure it has created and largely through the role played by the federal judiciary—has permitted only a fraction of those under sentence of death to be executed. As a matter of law and of constitutional principle, then, the state now stands between the majority of its citizens who favor executions and the demands of those who are under sentence of death that the rights of these offenders—many of whom have engaged in criminal acts of the most harmful and most heinous types you could imagine—to due process and equal protection under the law be protected. To be sure, those who opppose the death penalty are convinced that the state has played too permissive or passive a role in this area. They seek an end to all executions, and they believe that a reasonable reading of the Constitution demands this result. In contrast, those favoring the death penalty reach an entirely opposite conclusion. They seek an end to what they perceive to be endless delays, and they believe that the goal of justice will only be achieved by carrying out the sentences they view as having been imposed lawfully. The state has accepted neither of these polar points of view. Instead, it demands that the fundamental rights of even this especially harmful category of offenders to challenge the appropriateness of their sentences be protected.

In any event, I hope that some of what has been said in the previous paragraphs emphasizes how the subject matter of penology is of significance to all of us. Apart from my view that it is an interesting area of study in a purely academic way, crime and our responses to it play a role in our everyday lives in telling us something about the quality of the society in which we are participants and, on a still more abstract level, in allowing us to better understand the relationship that exists between the state and its citizens.

THE PLAN FOR WHAT IS TO FOLLOW

It would be unrealistic to expect that so brief a book as this could do justice to the broad range of topics that have stimulated the interest of criminologists over the years. I make no claim that it can or will. To the contrary, the fact of the matter is that virtually all of the issues to which we devote our attention could be and have been the focus of one or more book-length treatments in and of themselves. Our discussion is thus very selective and in some ways more superficial than some readers would prefer. Remember, however, that the goal we pursue does not call for an in-depth consideration of the entire field of penology or of the entire body of relevant theory and research that has apeared since the discipline of criminology began to take form some two hundred years ago. Instead, the goal is to introduce interested but beginning students to penology to some of the most significant and perplexing problems with which penologists are dealing today.

Pursuing that limited purpose, of course, requires attentiveness to some fact, figures, specific research studies, and particular theoretical formulations. That attentiveness, in turn, makes some portions of this book look much like an abbreviated version of a conventional textbook. But it is not a textbook, and it should not be used as one. Its real purpose is to address some critically important penological concerns that are of special significance not only to criminologists and penologists but also to those who are responsible for the formulation of those social and legal policies which shape our reactions to criminal and delinquent behavior.

For better or for worse, a clear majority of the topics to which our attention is given are not purely criminological—at least not if one understands criminology to be a behavioral science that is devoted to the objective, systematic, and empirical (i.e., scientific) study of crime. Materials, for example, from the disciplines of history, law, and philosophy cannot be ignored. Perhaps more important, no effort is made to pretend either that there is some matter-of-fact answer to the questions being posed by contemporary penologists or that penologists have come forward with two or more equally sound answers. Such an approach is commonly—though I think almost always unsuccessfully—taken by authors of textbooks. Their intent is often said to be "a presentation of the facts and nothing but the facts." Their claim, which I usually find to be little more than a pretense, is that they studiously avoid coloring such "factual presentations" with their own personal or professional judgments and opinions.

My rather different purpose here does not require that I make any such claims or advance any such pretenses. Indeed, in much of what follows we will encounter issues for which no obvious resolution exists and questions for which no precise answers have been found. Part of the objective, therefore, is to convince readers that criminologists in general and penologists in particular concern themselves with a host of perplexing and important topics, that those specialists sharply disagree with regard to what should or should not be done in the areas of social and legal policy, and above all that each reader can and should develop an informed opinion of his or her own. To leave such matters as defining what should or should not be defined as a crime, what should or should not be accepted as being the proper goals of punishment, who should or should not be punished, and whether or not there should be limits on the methods of punishment on which we rely (e.g., Should we retain or abolish the death penalty?) to the so-called "experts" is absolutely foolish. Sometimes experts can provide us with important information about both what is and what is likely to be if we adopt a particular means of resolving a particular problem, but they cannot and should not be given the power to tell us what should be. Being skeptical about the pronouncements of experts may well be an important indicator of both intelligence and mental health.

Unfortunately, I think, we too often misunderstand or ignore this reality. We permit politicians and lawyers and judges and correctional practitioners—and sometimes even criminologists—to tell us what we should do regarding penal policy and practice. Despite the nature of our political system and the power it confers on individual citizens, we give away our power to the "experts" based on little more than their claims to expertise and, perhaps, because of our own unwillingness to become informed and then act on the basis of our informed opinions. (Seldom, of course, do we refrain from acting on the basis of uninformed opinions, but much of the same could be said of the politicians and lawyers and judges and correctional practitioners—and, yes, often of criminologists—whose claims to "expert status" we seem so inclined to accept uncritically.) If any of the discussion to follow aids in the development of informed opinions, my real goal in writing will have been achieved.

General statements of the purpose of what is attempted here aside, here is an overview of what is to come. First, the next chapter is devoted to a brief review of what crime and punishment are and are not. We concern ourselves with how criminal behavior differs from other types of what are believed to be harmful acts, with some basic methods we often use to categorize types of crimes, and with how penologists, philosophers, and others have attempted to justify the right of the state to impose punishment on its citizens. Particular attention is devoted to retributive, utilitarian, and rehabilitative perspectives on the purposes of punishment.

The foundation provided by Chapters 1 and 2 is added to by the materials in Chapter 3. There we encounter a general overview of the origins, historical development, and present status of penology in the United States. Included in that chapter is a review of basic facts and figures regarding the volume of crime in the United States, the selective movement of cases through the criminal justice system, the number and characteristics of those presently under correctional supervision, and the resources now being made available to correctional practitioners.

Background information on the nature, history, and present status of penology having been provided in the first three chapters, the focus of our discussion narrows considerably as we move into the next two chapters. The intent of both chapters is to identify contemporary issues in penology that have attracted special public and/or professional attention. Chapter 4 focuses attention on a major conflict that is now transforming the field of penology in a host of ways. The conflict is linked to a heated debate taking place between advocates of the so-called *rehabilitative model* and various versions of what is commonly referred to as the *justice model*. Because neither the present status nor the probable future of penology can be understood until a thorough understanding of these two opposing perspectives has been reached, an entire chapter is devoted to a review and critical assessment of these two models.

Finally, Chapter 5 covers two topics that deal with the most extreme methods of punishment that can be employed within our system of criminal justice: imprisonment and capital punishment. Included in the discussion of prisons is a consideration of the role of prisons as what are often referred to as "people-processing organizations" and the plight of those who are sentenced to do time in our prison systems. If it does nothing else, the coverage of prison-based concerns should make it clear that the likelihood of our being able to rely on prisons as organizations within which meaningful changes in attitudes, values, and behavior can be achieved is minimal. Attention then shifts to an examination of capital punishment. I suspect that no single feature of penology has stimulated as much controversy as what we continue to find taking place between those who are unalterably opposed to capital punishment under any set of circumstances and those who view the death penalty as a fully appropriate means of dealing with some categories of offenders. It is hoped that the overview of the death penalty provided in Chapter 5 will provide an objective assessment of the history, utility, and present legal status of the death penalty in the United States.

DISCUSSION QUESTIONS

In what specific ways do you feel we can reasonably distinguish between the types of conduct that should be handled as a matter of private law versus those that should be dealt with as a matter of public law?

How can you account for the fact that some harmful behavior is prohibited by criminal law while other types of equally or even more harmful behavior escape criminalization?

NOTE

1. *Rummel v. Estelle* is an important case for those who are interested in the constitutional limits of legal sanctions as well as one that illustrates several points I attempt to make in this chapter. It is, however, important to avoid misleading readers by making more of it than it deserves. First of all, there is a significant series of cases—including *Weems v. United States*, 217 U.S. 349 (1910); *Trop v. Dulles*, 356 U.S. 86 (1958); *Robinson v. California*, 370 U.S. 660 (1962); and *Coker v. Georgia*, 433 U.S. 584 (1977)—that reflect the willingness of the Supreme Court to view legislative determinations regarding appropriate punishment as flatly unconstitutional. Furthermore, only a few years after *Rummel* was decided, another very similar case came before the Court in *Solem v. Helm*, 103 S.Ct. 3001 (1983). That case involved a South Dakota defendant, Jerry Helm, who had received a sentence of life imprisonment under South Dakota's habitual offender statute. Although Helm had a somewhat longer criminal record, all of his offenses had been nonviolent felonies. Unlike the Texas statute under which Rummel was sentenced, the South Dakota law permitted no possibility of early

release on parole for habitual offenders who had received sentences of life imprisonment. Justice Powell, in delivering the opinion of the Court, concluded his analysis of the case by observing: "The Constitution requires us to examine Helm's sentence to determine if it is proportionate to his crime. Applying objective criteria, we find that Helm has received the penultimate sentence for relatively minor criminal conduct....We concluded that his sentence is significantly disproportionate to his crime, and is therefore prohibited by the Eighth Amendment" (103 S.Ct. 3013).

2

CRIME AND PUNISHMENT

We have established that the major focus of criminologists who specialize in penology is the objective and systematic study of that special category of reactions to those who have been convicted of crimes that is dictated by the provisions of criminal law. The temptation is to move immediately to a consideration of such specific forms of reactions as probation, imprisonment, the death penalty, parole, and community-based rehabilitation initiatives. To do so, however, would be premature. First, some preliminary attention must be devoted to basic definitional issues. Precisely what do we mean when we say that something is a crime, that someone is a criminal, and that a person should be punished for his or her violation of a criminal law? More important, and quite apart from the specific method of punishment we may choose to rely on in a given case, what objectives do we have in mind when we permit or encourage the state to impose punishment of any kind on one of its citizens?

These limited concerns are the object of our attention in this chapter. Initially we give brief definitions of several very basic terms and concepts. We then pursue a more detailed examination of three basic perspectives that have been advanced by those who have concluded that at least some types of punishment for some kinds of offenders can be justified on moral and/or practical grounds.

DEFINING CRIMES, CRIMINALS, AND PUNISHMENT

To begin with, our concern is limited largely to behavior that is said to be in violation of the particular type of public law known as criminal law. We need to devote a modest amount of time to identifying basic categories of offenses that one finds in our body of criminal law and examining how definitions of those offenses are put together. From the very beginning, however, one point must be made as emphatically as possible. The making, modifying, and applying of criminal law must be thought of as outcomes in a continuing struggle between classes and groups within the population who strive to have their special viewpoints supported by the full power of the state. The making, modifying, and applying of law are thus outcomes of a political process and are clear indicators of who has been able to shape that political process (see, e.g., Chambliss and Seidman, 1982; Thomas and Hepburn, 1983: 38-74). Criminal law prohibits some forms of behavior that few of us would think of as especially harmful; it also prohibits many other forms of behavior that most of us think should be dealt with by relying on various types of private law remedies. At the same time, criminal law leaves untouched a vast array of exceedingly harmful types of behavior—especially harmful acts that involve governmental agencies and corporations.

We can and should make our own judgments regarding what should be the proper basis for making, modifying, and applying the provisions of criminal law. We must recognize, however, that criminal law is as much a political document as it is a reflection of firmly and widely held moral principles. As we turn our attention to such topics as how to define and justify punishment, it can be too easy to begin thinking of criminal law as something that contains an inherently good set of moral ideals that all reasonable people should support. Falling into that tempting trap, I think, should be studiously avoided. Our body of law may or may not reveal such moral ideals in each and every one of its component parts. Whether it does this well or poorly, however, does not alter one simple fact of life: *All law, private as well as public, is inherently and invariably the product of a political process.* As such it may serve either the common good or the particular interests of an adequately influential portion of the population. Thus, when later in this chapter you encounter a discussion of such notions as, "Offenders deserve to be punished in proportion to the harm caused by their criminal conduct," you would be prudent to remember how that conduct came to be defined as criminal. Otherwise, you may unknowingly take the politically conservative and (I think) naive position that all criminal law is good criminal law and that any violation of criminal law deserves to be condemned by all who are decent and moral citizens.

The politics of criminal law aside, criminal law can be broken down into many different categories. There are crimes against persons, crimes against property, crimes against the public order, and many others. One fairly general three-part categorization—*felonies, misdemeanors,* and *infractions*—is what we need to deal with here. A felony may be roughly defined as a serious criminal offense for which the maximum possible sentence (and not, for example, the minimum sentence or the sentence actually imposed by a trial court) is in excess of one year of confinement in a state or federal prison. A misdemeanor is a less serious criminal offense for which the maximum period of confinement is generally less than one year of confinement in a local jail facility. An infraction is the least serious offense—most criminologists prefer to avoid even defining it as a crime—for which the maximum sentence authorized by law is a fine. Most of our concern in this and other chapters will be with reactions to those offenses that criminal law defines as being especially serious (i.e., felonies).

Shifting our attention from defining categories of crimes to defining distinctions between criminals and noncriminals is not as simple as it might seem. The temptation, of course, is to say that a criminal is any person who engages in conduct defined by the state as a felony or misdemeanor. That, however, would be a very misleading definition of a criminal. This is because the burden placed on the state when it prosecutes someone for a crime almost always goes beyond the mere requirement that it prove "beyond a reasonable doubt" that the defendant engaged in behavior prohibited by a criminal law. Instead, its burden is to prove each and every element in the definition of the offense. The elements in the definitions of crimes are simply the building blocks that, taken together, make a complete definition. There are often three such elements. The behavioral *element*—usually referred to as *actus reus,* which means the prohibited conduct—is commonly accompanied by a *mens rea* element and sometimes by a *scienter* element. *Mens rea* refers to the mental status of the actor at the time of the alleged offense. Roughly defined, it means that the offender did something prohibited by criminal law—or failed to do something required by criminal law—intentionally. *Scienter* refers to the special knowledge the alleged offender may be required to have had at the time of the offense if he or she is to be defined as a criminal.

An example or two should clarify the point. Florida law, for instance, defines a criminal assault to be "an intentional, unlawful threat by word or act to do violence to the person of another, coupled with an apparent ability to do so, and doing some act which creates a well-founded fear in such other person that such violence is imminent" (Florida Statutes Annotated, 784.011). This is perhaps the most common form of criminl law. It describes the prohibited conduct (i.e., the *actus reus* element) and the state of mind an offender is assumed to have had when he or she engaged in that conduct (i.e., the *mens rea* element). The state must prove both that the behavior took place and that the behavior was intentional.

Here, of course, the *mens rea* element is broadly defined. It is an illustration of what is meant by the term *general criminal intent.* That is not always the case, however. Florida, for example, defines burglary to be "the entering or remaining in a structure or conveyance with the intent to commit an offense therein" (Florida Statutes Annotated, 810.02). Thus, a prosecutor would have a somewhat higher burden regarding a burglary offense than he or she would confront regarding an assault offense. Intentionally entering the home of another, for instance, would be only part of the burden. It also would have to be proven that the unlawful entry was done with the purpose of committing some other offense. This is a rough illustration of what is meant by *specific criminal intent*.

Neither the assault nor the burglary offense includes a *scienter* element, but consider the following definition of bigamy: "Whoever knowingly marries the husband or wife of another person, knowing him or her to be the spouse of another person, shall be guilty of a felony of the third degree" (Florida Statutes Annotated, 826.03). The distinction should be obvious. A successful prosecution for the offense of bigamy would require more than a demonstration that one person intentionally married another person even though the other person was still married to someone else. The state would have to bear the additional burden of showing that the alleged offender knew that the person he or she married was still married to another.

While space does not permit pursuing this issue further, it should be clear that there is more to defining a criminal than looking at his or her behavior. The possibility always exists that the alleged offender fully intended to do whatever he or she may be charged with having done but that he or she did so with a legally acceptable justification, defense, or excuse (e.g., infancy, self-defense, defense of another person, mistake of fact, insanity, duress or coercion, necessity, and many more; Fletcher, 1978: 759-876; Gardner and Manian, 1980: 112-158; Thomas and Bishop, 1986). The law, for instance, excuses what would otherwise be criminal behavior when it reflects a reasonable effort on the part of a person to defend himself or herself or to defend another person. The following illustration from Florida law is fairly typical of how such excuses are defined:

> A person is justified in the use of force, except deadly force, against another when and to the extent that such conduct is necessary to defend himself against such other's imminent use of unlawful force....He is justified in the use of deadly force only if he reasonably believes that such force is necessary to prevent imminent death or great bodily harm to himself or another or to prevent the imminent commission of a forcible felony [Florida Statutes Annotated, 776.012].

A criminal may thus be defined as any culpable person convicted by a criminal court of any action or inaction prohibited by law and punishable by the state as a felony or misdemeanor. However, it is important to recognize that this is a legal rather than a criminological definition (e.g., Thomas and Hepburn, 1983: 9-36). In most areas of criminological inquiry the appropriate focus of our attention is on the large number of persons who engage in criminal behavior rather than on the far smaller number who are apprehended, tried, and convicted. This is even true of some aspects of penological research. Most commonly, however, penologists deal with the nature and consequences of penal sanctions that have been imposed on convicted offenders. They must therefore make a special effort to remember, for example, that criminal law is the product of a political process, that many if not most criminal victimizations are not reported to law enforcement agencies, that the vast majority of reported offenses—perhaps 80 percent of all reported serious felonies—do not result in an arrest, and that a significant proportion of arrest fail to result in either successful or unsuccessful prosecutions. To ignore these and other factors that influence the criminal justice process and to thereby assume that those sentenced by our criminal courts are something other than a very atypical category of people is to make a fatal mistake.

One additional concept needs to be defined before we move ahead—punishment. Defining it is not especially difficult, but doing so can be confusing simply because it is a term that is used so frequently and so broadly in everyday language. Here, however, we give it a very narrow meaning. *Punishment is any lawfully imposed pain, suffering, or loss of otherwise available rights confronted by an actor as a consequence of his or her culpable criminal action or inaction.* Punishment is thus something very different from, for example, *informal sanctions* (i.e., negative responses we make to those who violate informal rules or standards of the type represented by standards of social etiquette) or *formal sanctions* (i.e., negative reactions we have to those who violate the more formal and most commonly written rules and regulations of, for instance, social and religious organizations, educational institutions, corporations, and so on). Punishment also is not a term that we would use were we dealing with the special set of formal sanctions that we call *legal sanctions* when we work in the broad area of either private law or some noncriminal categories of public law (i.e., international law). Instead, it is the very special term we apply only in those contexts where we find "lawfully imposed pain, suffering, or loss of otherwise available rights confronted by an

actor as a consequence of his or her culpable criminal action or inaction.'' To make the same point a bit differently, punishment is not a
term that we reserve for some deprivation that may be imposed on
an actor because he or she violated some general normative standard
or rule (i.e., formal or informal sanctions) or even because he or she
violated some provision of law (i.e., legal sanctions). Instead, it is
what an actor may lawfully confront when he or she experiences some
deprivation lawfully imposed *by the state* for violating a law created
by the state which defines his or her conduct as an offense *against the
state* rather than as an offense against some private party.

THE PRIMARY PURPOSES OF PUNISHMENT

Having established a working definition of punishment, including
definitions of the forms of behavior (i.e., crimes) and types of persons
(i.e., criminals) said to deserve punishment, we must now identify the
primary purposes of punishment. What is it, in other words, that we
seek to do or gain when we impose punishment on offenders? What
goals do we (rightly or wrongly) believe that we can achieve by means
of punishment? When we seek to pursue more than a single goal—as
when, for instance, we hope both to rehabilitate an offender we have
placed in prison and to use that offender's confinement as an example
designed to deter other persons from similar unlawful conduct—are
those multiple goals consistent with or contradictory to one another?

These questions push us toward a philosophical and conceptual
swamp from which we would never be able to escape were we to deal
with them as thoroughly as perhaps we should. They have been the
subject of heated debate for centuries (for more detailed considerations see, for example, Pincoffs, 1966; Hart, 1968; Gerber and
McAnany, 1972; Kaufman, 1973; Gross and von Hirsch, 1981;
Thomas and Hepburn, 1983: 416-457). Risking a degree of over-
simplification that would certainly be offensive to those with special
interests in the moral philosophy of punishment, we can make some
quick and crude distinctions among general orientations toward the justification of punishment. This can be done by contrasting the basic
characteristics of *retributive, utilitarian,* and *rehabilitative perspectives.*

Punishment as Retribution

Simply summarized, retributivism, which is often said to be the
oldest means of justifying punishment, encourages us to ignore how

or if punishment may influence the future attitudes, values, beliefs, and behavior of those who are punished (see, e.g., Pincoffs, 1966; Honderich, 1971; Murphy, 1973; Feinberg and Gross, 1975; Bedau, 1978, 1984). Such a future orientation is said to carry with it the danger that we will come to think of those who are punished merely as a means to an end and not as fully responsible people whose rights we are obligated to protect. Immanuel Kant made this quite clear nearly two centuries ago in his *Philosophy of Law:*

> Punishment can never be administered merely as a means for promoting another Good ... but must in all cases be imposed only because the individual on whom it is inflicted has committed a crime. For one man ought never to be dealt with merely as a means subservient to the purpose of another. ... Against such treatment his Inborn Personality has a Right to protect him, although he may be condemned to lose his Civil Personality. ... Even if a Civil Society resolved to dissolve itself with the consent of all its members ... the last Murderer lying in the prison ought to be executed before the resolution was carried out. This ought to be done in order that every one may realize the desert of his deeds, and the bloodguiltiness may not remain upon the people; for otherwise they might all be regarded as participators in the murder as a public violation of justice [quoted in Honderich, 1971: 22].

The proper approach, retributivists argue, is to look backward in time to the seriousness and harmfulness of the offense that has been committed and to the moral blameworthiness of the offender. Should we find that harm has been done by a person who has no morally acceptable defense or excuse, then it is said that we have an obligation to punish the offender. Justice is said to demand such a response to those who choose to violate agreed upon rules of behavior and to thereby do harm to their fellow citizens. As summarized by Bedau (1978: 602-603), the retributivist accepts the premise that "the justification for punishing persons is that the return of suffering for moral evil voluntarily done is itself just or morally good."

A retributive point of view includes at least two very important concepts: the principle of just desert and the principle of proportionality. Both relate to the retributivist's firm conviction that the amount or type of punishment we can justly impose on blameworthy offenders is neither more nor less than what they deserve given the harmfulness of their conduct. Offenders who receive more or less than their just desert, therefore, would have been punished in a manner that would be offensive to the principle of proportionality.

Retributivists differ, however, in precisely how they would prefer to see their ideas translated into the provisions of criminal law. As Feinberg and Gross (1975: 4) observe:

> Retributivists are often understandably vague about the practical inter-
> pretations of the key notions of fittingness, proportion, and moral
> gravity. Sometimes aesthetic analogies are employed (such as matching
> and clashing colors, or harmonious and dissonant chords). Some
> retributivists, including Immanuel Kant, attempt to apply the ancient
> principle of *lex talionis* (the law of retaliation), that the punishment
> should match the crime not only in the degree of harm inflicted on the
> victim, but also in the mode and manner of infliction: fines for larceny,
> physical beating for battery, capital punishment for murder. Other
> retributivists, however, explicitly reject the doctrine of retaliation in
> kind; hence that doctrine is better treated as a logically independent
> thesis commonly associated with retributivism than as an essential com-
> ponent of the theory.

At the extreme, then, one could take an "in kind" or *lex talionis* version of this perspective and thereby demand the proverbial "eye for an eye, tooth for a tooth, life for a life" solution to the problem of determining in what way or how much to punish. So literal a translation of what is meant by just desert can cause some obvious problems, however. What, for example, would a rapist "deserve"? Or the murderer of another person's child? Or the arsonist who burns the home of another? Or a terrorist?

A somewhat "softer" retributive viewpoint defines the idea of just desert as a *defining principle,* "a principle which if adopted as the purpose to be served by punishment would give the exact sanction to be imposed" (Morris, 1982: 182; see also Hart, 1968; Packer, 1968; Morris, 1974: 59-84). Even if one thinks of just deserts as something shaped by a defining principle, the difficulties of creating retributively based sentencing policies are considerable. Few people would ever agree on precisely what sentence an offender should receive for a given criminal offense. This explains in part why the idea of just deserts is often thought of as providing what Morris (1982: 183) and others describe as a *limiting principle* that, "though it would rarely tell us the exact sanction to be imposed ... would nevertheless give us the outer limits of leniency and severity which should not be exceeded." One might thus argue that retributive principles require that those convicted of a particular crime must receive no less than a sentence of x but no more than a sentence of y. Any sentence within such a range presumably would have a firm justification.

Much of our criminal law draws in part on retribution as a limiting principle. One illustration of this is provided by the holding of the U.S. Supreme Court in *Coker v. Georgia* (433 U.S. 584, 1977). There the court held that sentences of death could not be imposed on defendants who had been convicted of the rape of adult women—or of any person and perhaps even for any offense that did not involve an act of criminal homicide—because so harsh a sentence would be disproportionate to the offense committed. In other words, it would be above the outer acceptable limit of severity. Dealing with the idea of retribution as a limiting principle, however, still leaves us with a very thorny problem: How do we go about the business of establishing the upper and lower limits of punishment? How do we create an equation that will permit us to compute each offender's just deserts in a way that will not be offensive to the basic principles of proportionality?

The answers to these questions, unfortunately, have never been put forward in an acceptable fashion (e.g., Gibbs, 1980; Bedau, 1984). While it seems obvious that it would be foolish to rely on retributivism as a source of specific punishments (i.e., to see this perspective as one that contains defining principles), trying to understand retributivism as a source of limiting principles seems only to beg the question. We still have no way of saying—at least not with any true confidence—what a burglary or rape or act of bribery is "worth" when we have established that we are dealing with a blameworthy offender and are seeking guidance regarding the sentence that should be imposed. Having an interval that is thought to mark the limits of just punishment may lessen the likelihood of our being unjust. It may even permit us, as Morris (1982) and others argue, to pursue other purposes of punishment (e.g., rehabilitation) so long as we pursue them within the limits of what we can justify on retributive grounds. But it tells us little or nothing about the just value of either the minimum or the maximum punishment. As a matter of policymaking, therefore, we are left in the position of having justice in sentencing being equal to little more than the will of a particular legislative body at a particular point in time.

Justice thus becomes the product of a political process, a process that is shaped by a broad spectrum of variables other than—and often contrary to—notions like just desert and proportionality. The only major check on such political definitions comes from the decisions of our appellate courts. Of course, this type of review is not without its own fundamental problems. The appellate courts, including the U.S. Supreme Court, are hardly apolitical creatures. Indeed, appointments to the Supreme Court are among the most obvious and influential illustrations of political power that can be found within our system of government. Furthermore, appellate courts are inclined to defer to "legislative wisdom," "principles of federalism," "judicial restraint," and a host of other justifications that permit them to conclude, as the Supreme Court did in *Rummel v. Estelle* (445 U.S. 275, 1980), that "the length of the sentence imposed is purely a matter of legislative prerogative." This has the effect of the courts ignoring altogether the justice of the lower limits of punishments provided for in our body of criminal law and taking a contrary position regarding the upper limits of punishment only in very unusual circumstances (e.g., *Weems v. United States*, 217 U.S. 349, 1910; *Trop v. Dulles*, 356 U.S. 86, 1958; *Coker v. Georgia*, 433 U.S. 584, 1977).

In light of the preceding discussion, I have grave reservations about the moral or ethical as well as the practical virtues of retributivism as a means of justifying the imposition of any particular punishment on any particular offender. True, on a very general theoretical level each of us would probably appreciate and perhaps even accept the notion that guilty persons deserve to be punished for the harm they have caused and that the punishment they receive should be no greater and no less than they deserve. But imagine trying to translate such generalities into a concrete criminal code within the context of our (or any other) political system. The hard reality is that nothing in a retributive point of view provides us with standards by means of which the "scales of justice" can be balanced. Indeed, even if one were to take the relatively extreme position that we could fix the upper and lower limits of just deserts by empirical measures of the "will of the governed," the task we would confront would be impossibly complex. For instance, what proportion or percentage of citizens would we require to endorse a given punishment or range of punishments as just? Half? Two-thirds? And what if we agreed to accept as a lower limit of just deserts a sentence that would be morally offensive to half of our population were it to be any more lenient and as an upper limit a sentence that would be morally offensive to half of our population were it to be any harsher? Would that really resolve our problem?

Perhaps. But on the basis of what types of information would all citizens be asked to express their moral beliefs? The nature of the offense committed? The amount of harm done? What kinds of harm—physical, financial, reputational, and so on—qualify as that which should be considered in the creation of our novel body of criminal law? What about the social, economic, or political position occupied by a culpable offender at the time of his or her violation of our laws? Is, for instance, a fine of $500.00 equally appropriate for both poor and wealthy offenders? Is a year in a penitentiary equally punitive both for a young, unskilled single man and for a middle-aged married woman who is the sole source of support for three young children? And what of the offender's past conduct? Do we ask all citizens how much—if at all—prior criminal convictions are worth as they go about the business of setting up their retributive system of justice?

The list of questions, of course, could be made much, much longer. The obvious reality, however, is that "doing justice" as a retributivist is far from easy. Retributivists wax eloquent in defense of their conviction that the guilty deserve and must receive no more and no less than what their blameworthy conduct deserves. Fine. Perhaps they have a valid point. But they really tell us little more than when punishment is appropriate and at whom it should be directed. Once we have our collective hands on someone whose morally blameworthy conduct in violation of criminal law has brought harm to one or more of us, retributivists have little if anything to tell us about the type or degree of punishment we should choose. Indeed, Bedau (1984) has observed that two "equally pure" retributivists could come forward with very different recommendations regarding the just deserts of the same offender, and neither they nor we would have a logical or theoretical means of determining which recommendation was better. Retributivists thus assume the role of something like a travel agent to whom we have gone to get information about a vacation we would like to take. They tell us much about a place we might like to visit and why it is worth visiting, and they are quite convincing. Then they are forced to admit that they have no idea whatsoever about the route we should take in trying to reach the destination they have described in such attractive terms.

The Utility Value of Punishment

A quest for means of justifying punishment, of course, need not lead us to look backward in time, assess the blameworthiness of an offender, measure the harmfulness of his or her conduct, and then impose whatever punishment we can justify on retributive grounds. Utilitarianism provides us with a clear example of an influential alternative—one that is forward-looking rather than backward-looking (e.g., Rawls, 1956, 1971; Beccaria, 1963; Bentham, 1975; Honderich, 1971; Ezorsky, 1972).

Utilitarians think of the causes of human conduct in a way that can be roughly summarized as follows: Humans are amoral creatures who are primarily motivated by self-interest and who, given their inherent ability to evaluate the probable consequences of their behavior before they choose between available behavioral options, will choose those behavioral options that are expected to bring the greatest benefits at the lowest cost. Crime prevention, therefore, simply requires that actors be convinced that the risks and costs associated with criminal choice are so high that such choices are contrary to self-interest. In his influential *An Introduction to the Principles of Morals and Legislation,* for example, Bentham (1975: 29) argues that the temptation to commit offenses is strongly related to the profits the offense might yield, so "the quantum of the punishment must rise with the profit of the offense."

In effect, then, if we wish to control or prevent crime, we must simply convince everyone that "crime does not pay" through our ability to manipulate relevant aspects of punishment. Convincing does not necessarily involve the contention that punishment will influence human behavior directly. Instead, punishment is said to influence the perception of risk (i.e., the perceived costs associated with unlawful acts), and these perceptions of risk in turn shape the nature of the behavior in which we choose to involve ourselves (or, of course, that we choose to avoid).

The most important features of punishment from this vantage point would certainly include its *swiftness* (i.e., the amount of time elapsing between the commission of a crime and our reactions to the offender), its *certainty* (i.e., the likelihood that those who violate the law will confront some legal reaction), and its *severity* (i.e., the amount of punishment imposed on those who are apprehended). Bentham and other utilitarian philosphers are well aware of how difficult it might be to manipulate all three of these characteristics of punishment. The general hypotheis, however, is that a deficiency in one area could be compensated for by strength in another. Thus, to take only the most obvious and common possibility, when swift and certain punishment seems difficult or impossible, one can always fall back on severity. To quote once again from Bentham (1975: 30): "Want of certainty must be made up in magnitude....Punishment must be further increased in point of magnitude, in proportion as it falls short of proximity."

While crime prevention is the most obvious general goal of punishment from the perspective of utilitarians, there are any number of more specific purposes. The most important of these are *general deterrence, specific deterrence, marginal deterrence,* and *incapacitation.* Some care should be taken to avoid confusing these goals with one another. General deterrence refers to the effect of punishment on the subsequent perceptions of risk among persons other than those who actually receive punishment. (Do those who consider the potential benefits of selling illegal drugs avoid doing so because they have learned that such behavior carries excessive and unacceptable risks through their awareness of the punishment that has been imposed on drug dealers in the past?) Specific deterrence refers to the effect of punishment on the subsequent perceptions of risk of those who are punished. (Do those who have been punished for drug dealing in the past avoid such conduct today because the punishment they have encountered has taught them that the risks of such behavior are greater than its potential rewards?) Marginal deterrence has to do with incremental increases in the deterrent effects of punishment that we realize when we elevate the level of punishment from one level to a higher level. (If the minimum sentence for drug dealing was raised from, for example, four years in prison to eight years in prison, would the rate of violations of the applicable drug law drop in some significant fashion?) Finally, incapacitation, a goal that is altogether unrelated to risk perceptions, refers to our ability to reduce the incidence of unlawful conduct by dealing with offenders in such a way as to reduce or eliminate their opportunities to violate the law. (A person serving a prison sentence on a drug dealing conviction lacks the opportunity to sell drugs—at least outside the prison in which he or she is confined—during his or her period of confinement even if that punishment has no influence whatsoever on his or her behavior upon release from prison.) Obviously, then, one could achieve any one of these goals of punishment without being able to achieve the others, but the contention would be that the overall volume of crime would be reduced if even one of them were to fall within our grasp.

Putting aside the individual goals of punishment favored by the utilitarians, emphasis should be given to how different this perspective is from the retributive point of view. Retributivists greatly dislike the idea of seeking future benefits from punishment. They see such efforts as reflecting an inclination to treat people as mere objects and perhaps to fall into the trap of concluding that the end (crime prevention) justifies the means (virtually any amount or type of punishment). This means-ends reasoning, say the retributivists, could result in offenders receiving either less or more than their just deserts.

This appears to be a fair criticism. Utilitarians claim that no more punishment should be imposed than is absolutely necessary if we are to achieve the "proper" purposes of punishment. Utilitarians as a general rule are also far more opposed to such extreme punishments as the death penalty than is true of retributivists. However, one can imagine the possibility of very serious offenses requiring modest punishments and very minor offenses requiring fairly harsh punishments were all punishments to be dictated by some extension of utilitarian logic.

This feature of a utilitarian perspective has proven to be a significant problem when the viewpoint has been translated into actual social and legal policy. You should be able to imagine how this has happened. A legislative body identifies a type of behavior that it would like to prevent. The behavior is defined as a crime, and some type or range of punishment is set forth in a new statute. Time passes. The law is applied repeatedly. The behavior persists. What should be done? The question is often answered by the legislative body concluding that the type or range of punishment it provided for initially is insufficient to persuade offenders from engaging in the prohibited conduct, so the punishment is made harsher. The behavior still persists. The punishment is made still harsher. The cycle can go on and on, and often this happens without any attention whatsoever being given to the very real possibility that the theory of punishment is itself defective. The history of our efforts to control the manufacture, distribution, and use of various prescription and nonprescription drugs is perhaps the most obvious example of this pattern of legal reactions (e.g., Lindesmith, 1965; Duster, 1970).

The problem, of course, is that the classical statements of the utilitarian perspective are too simplistic. The image of a person carefully weighing and evaluating the benefits and costs of criminal and noncriminal options before acting may have some merit with regard to some types of offenses. However, much criminal conduct involves, among other things, people making choices when they are angry, when they are confronted with extreme deprivation, when they lack access to conventional opportunities, or when their capacity for calculating risks is diminished by their use of alcohol or other drugs. Much other criminal behavior is so spontaneous in nature that it involves little or no advance planning or contemplation. The utilitarian viewpoint seems unable to accept these or other common exceptions to its image of what makes us tick.

Further, the model tends to presuppose that all actors are aware of and carefully take into account the provisions of criminal law. This is often a premise that is hard to accept. Often, for example, I have encountered prison inmates who were fully aware at the time they committed such serious offenses as murder that they were certain to be apprehended. Indeed, some committed especially serious crimes like murder only then to turn themselves in to the police. Other considerations, however, prompted them to ignore altogether the certainty of harsh punishment. One such inmate, for example, had killed his wife after learning that she had been involved sexually with another man. His feeling was that her conduct was so totally offensive to his beliefs and moral standards that she had to be killed, so she was. He then tried unsuccessfully to kill himself. The point is that no legal threat would have persuaded this man to refrain from his criminal act. He felt, in effect, an obligation to what he perceived to be a higher moral authority than the law, and from his point of view he met that obligation.

Efforts to use punishment to achieve future benefits run afoul of many other more or less practical problems. The administration of criminal justice, for example, is relatively inefficient regarding the apprehension of offenders. Even with regard to what are often defined as the most serious types of felonious offenses, the likelihood of even as much as an arrest taking place is less than 20 percent. It would be hard to see such low probabilities of reaction as constituting a high risk. In fact, some research is now showing that those who come into contact with our juvenile and criminal justice systems may come to learn that the risk of punishment is lower than they once thought it to be (e.g., Thomas and Bishop, 1984). This means that reactions can diminish rather than elevate the perception of risk.

Another problem presents itself when we understand that punishment sometimes has the ability to create the very behavior it seeks to prevent. This can happen in at least two fairly obvious ways. Consider first the sort of problem we encounter with regard to some types of arson or drug offenses. An offender is apprehended and punished. Are potential offenders thereby deterred? Perhaps. But it is also true that the costs associated with, for example, hiring an arsonist or buying drugs increase, and this in turn increases the profits associated with such offenses. Individuals not previously attracted to the offenses may then come to see them as more attractive. Second, punishment certainly has the ability to produce contradictory results. Just as it might increase the punished person's perception of risk, it can also decrease his or her access to noncriminal opportunities (e.g., Schwartz and Skolnick, 1962). If punishment so stigmatizes offenders that, for example, they have few or no employment opportunities in the conventional world, they may find themselves in a position that provides them with decreased conventional but perhaps increased criminal opportunities.

In short, adopting a utilitarian perspective on punishment is hardly a move that resolves all of the questions that we need to resolve. Like the retributivists, the utilitarians contend that only the guilty deserve to be punished. Few of us would argue with that limitation on the use of the power of the state. Unlike the retributivists, the utilitarians do not think of punishment as a way of looking backward in time and doing what needs to be done to balance the scales of justice. Instead, they look to the future with the demand that the punishment of guilty persons must serve one or more of the goals we associate with the overall objective of crime prevention.

But very much like the retributivists, the utilitarians do little more than tell us who deserves punishment and why we should tolerate their being punished. When it comes to guidelines regarding more or less precisely how judges charged with the obligation of imposing sentences should discharge their sentencing obligations, the utilitarians have little to offer. Furthermore, even if there were more to the utilitarian perspective than I have been able to find, those adopting it would have the obvious obligation to examine and evaluate on a continuous basis the ability of a given punishment to achieve the objective by reference to which the punishment was justified. Evaluations are done from time to time, but they are not routine agenda items for the criminal justice system, they reveal little to support the position advanced by the utilitarians, and they almost never result in even the slightest change being made in penal policy—other than, of course, providing ammunition for politicians who seem to enjoy making the already harsh provisions of our body of criminal law still harsher as they go about the obvious and transparent business of maintaining their individual bases of power.

The Rehabilitative Value of Punishment

It is imperative that a good deal of caution be employed in any effort to examine rehabilitation as a more or less independent justification for punishment. The term itself has come to mean many different things, and often—too often, I think—we have come to think of rehabilitative efforts as being so saintly and pure that to criticize them is to admit that one hates God, motherhood, apple pie, and whatever else may occupy the high ground of our society. At the risk of oversimplifying a very important issue—one to which we return early in Chapter 4—we can begin to understand this perspective on punishment by trying to distinguish it from the retributive and utilitarian viewpoints we have already reviewed.

One basic and fairly obvious distinction is that retributive and utilitarian statements about punishment have come primarily from scholars and practitioners whose intellectual ties have been to the fields of philosophy or law and whose most salient concern has been with creating a system of administering justice that was fair, reasonable, and equitable. To be sure, we have seen that the retributivists and utilitarians differ with one another in many important regards. The retributivists see the best of all possible worlds as one within which "doing justice" by guaranteeing that all offenders receive no more and no less than their just deserts is the dominant concern. The utilitarians differ in the important sense that "doing justice" involves efforts aimed at gaining future benefits from punishment (e.g., general deterrence, specific deterrence, and so on) and thereby achieving the general goal of crime prevention.

By and large, however, these two viewpoints are similar in two important ways. First, they view human actors as being fully responsible persons who have and who exercise the ability to choose between good and evil. Roughly, then, retributivists would punish offenders because they have chosen to do harm and therefore deserve to be punished in proportion to the harm they chose to cause. Utilitarians would punish the same offenders with the objective of decreasing the likelihood that either those or similar persons would choose to engage in any harmful conduct in the future. Second, largely because both retributivists and utilitarians imagine that their "free choice" explanation for human behavior is fully adequate, neither group has been especially concerned with features of the criminal justice process that unfold after the point at which a sentence has been imposed. They more or less imagine that the presumed benefits of punishment (giving each offender his or her just deserts for the retributivist and preventing crime for the utilitarians) will fall within our grasp if and when the "front end" of the criminal justice system operates in the manner they recommend.

Naturally, I am not suggesting that, for example, retributivists and utilitarians could care less about such things as prison conditions. That would be flatly untrue. Similarly, neither group would become hostile were those being punished to become involved in programs aimed at bettering them in some educational, physical, psychological, social, or vocational way. To choose but a single illustration, Jeremy Bentham (1975: 27-28), a leading advocate of utilitarianism, argues: "It is a great merit in punishment to contribute to the reformation of the offender, not only through fear of being punished again, but by a change in his character and habits." Retributivists, of course, would object were participation in such programs to either increase or decrease the amount of punishment to be received. Just deserts flow from harm caused by blameworthy conduct in the past and not by whatever positive actions an offender may take in the present. Similarly, utilitarians would have reason to object were program participation, for instance, to create a longer deprivation of liberty than was necessary to achieve their crime prevention goals. What I am suggesting is that the historical development of these two quite different perspectives on punishment reveals relatively little attention to the design or implementation of programs aimed at dealing with offenders beyond their considerable concern with sentencing policies.

Those who seek to justify punishment because they place primary importance on its value as a rehabilitative tool are a very different breed (e.g., Karpman, 1956; Menninger, 1968; Conrad and Schneider, 1980; Cullen and Gilbert, 1982). First, rather than having a fondness for law or philosophy, they have tended to cast their lot with the clinical disciplines (medicine, psychology, psychiatry, and so on) or the so-called "helping professions" (especially social work). Second, they flatly reject the hypothesis that most offenders chose to violate the law and are therefore blameworthy. Their contrary contention is that criminal behavior, and also noncriminal conduct, is caused by prior events and forces the identity of which can be established by careful scientific inquiry. Third, going well beyond what any cause-and-effect hypothesis requires, they argue that crime must be viewed in much the same way that we view a disease. Therefore, crime is said to be a symptom whose cause cries out for treatment—and certainly not as an offense that deserves punishment. Karpman (1973: 131) is among those whose work illustrates all of this quite clearly:

> Criminal psychodynamics sees criminality as basically a psychiatric, extra-legal problem. It does not see the criminal eye to eye with the public and the law as a vicious individual for whom the only treatment is punishment. ... It views the problems of right and wrong, of guilt and responsibility, or irresistible impulse not as a abstract concepts or transient trends in human behavior but as being deeply rooted in the basic biological make-up of man. It views criminality, however incidental it may seem on the surface, as a basic human expression having a long history and evolution and a pathology all its own. It sees in criminality a disease sui generis, a severe disease which, however, can be cured or prevented when and if proper psychotherapeutic measures are taken.

Realistically, then, those who support the rehabilitative approach do not provide us with a third major means of justifying punishment. Punishment only makes sense when one is dealing with offenders who are believed to be personally responsible for their unlawful conduct and the harm that such conduct has caused. As soon as one rejects the notion of personal responsibility, one must also reject the reasonableness of punishment. Perhaps, therefore, those accepting this viewpoint would be better described as people who seek to justify the right of the state to intervene in the lives of offenders and sometimes to deprive them of their liberty for some period of time. Intervention—not punishment—is justified because it provides society with an opportunity to treat a medical or quasi-medical condition that poses a risk to the welfare of others. Thought of in this fashion, of course, the duration of our "intervention" is not limited by what is deserved given the nature of the harm done or a desire to either deter or incapacitate. The lower and upper limits of intervention are set exclusively by the progress of the rehabilitative efforts that legitimized the intervention in the first place. Put more simply, the state is said to have an obligation to maintain control over criminal "patients" until their "disease" has been "cured." Offense seriousness, for example, comes to be defined as flatly irrelevant. Presumably some who have stolen automobiles can be cured quickly, while others may require a lengthy period of rehabilitation.

We shall direct our attention to the rehabilitative approach when we compare and contrast alternative perspectives on the role of our penal or correctional system in Chapter 4. For now it is sufficient to note that justifying what we do with, to, or for convicted offenders by referring to the rehabilitative value of our reactions has been no more successful or satisfying than relying on retributive or utilitarian approaches. Simply put, the persistent weaknesses of the rehabilitative model seem to stem from the invalidity of its most fundamental assertions. Those assertions include the following: (1) that crime is the consequence of influences other than individual choice, influences over which individual offenders have little or no control; (2) that our knowledge base regarding the true causes of and cures for crime is sufficiently sophisticated that we can establish its causes in individual cases and then prescribe a suitably effective treatment program; (3) that having diagnosed the causes of crime and prescribed appropriate reactions, we have the ability to monitor the progress of our therapeutic efforts well enough that we can establish when our "patients" have been "cured"; and (4) that we have sufficient control over relevant social, political, and legal processes that we can establish the specialized type of rehabilitative system within which we can do what needs to be done in the pursuit of the individualized treatment of offenders. Were one to sift through a huge literature on the various sorts of rehabilitative efforts we have made over the years, the harsh reality is that those efforts have been largely impotent (e.g., Bailey, 1966; Kassenbaum et al., 1971; Morris, 1974; Lerman, 1975; Lipton et al., 1975; and Riedel and Thornberry, 1978).

SUMMARY AND CONCLUSIONS

We have pursued three fairly matter-of-fact questions in this chapter. First, what kinds of persons warrant being classified as criminals within the context of our system of criminal justice? Second, when and if we conclude that punishment should be imposed on such persons, precisely what do we mean by the term "punishment"? Third, when and if punishment is said to be appropriate, in what fashion do we go about the business of creating sound and meaningful justifications for our reactions to offenders?

Regarding the first question, some general as well as some specific principles warrant emphasis. On a general level, it is important to recognize that the kinds of behavior required or prohibited by criminal law are not necessarily the kinds of behavior that are either especially harmful or that are perceived to be especially harmful. Definitions of crimes are instead the products of a political process. Sometimes that process accurately reflects the collective judgment of the vast majority of citizens. Often, however, it reflects the particular interests and preferences of those whose access to social, economic, or political power permits them to control the process by means of which law is created, modified, and applied in the everyday operation of our criminal justice system (see, e.g., Chambliss and Seidman, 1982; Thomas and Hepburn, 1983: 38-74). Therefore, it is imperative that we remember that those who are defined as criminals are believed to have violated a political standard. Such violations may or may not warrant moral condemnation. They may or may not have caused harm of the type that a majority of us view as properly falling within the scope of criminal law. They certainly do not include all of the sorts of behavior that a majority of us view as being harmful.

On a more specific level we have found that there is a good deal more to defining individuals as criminals than seems immediately apparent. Engaging in prohibited conduct (or refraining to engage in required conduct)—the *actus reus* element in the definition of a crime—is only part of what is often required. Usually it must also be proven that the violation was done with some type of criminal intent—the *mens rea* element—and often the burden of proof increases because of the requirement that the violation involves one who knowingly violated a provision of criminal law—the *scienter* element. Further, criminal responsibility or liability in our system of justice often vanishes because the alleged offender is able to come forward with a legally acceptable justification, defense, or excuse for his or her otherwise criminal conduct. Such means of avoiding criminal responsibility include, for instance, self-defense, defense of third persons, insanity, mistake of fact, entrapment, and many more. Further still, types of violations vary with regard to the legal definitions of their seriousness (i.e., felony offenses, misdemeanor offenses, and infractions). Most of our attention, of course, has been devoted to punishment and its supposed justifications. Special consideration was given to three major means of justifying punishment: retribution, crime prevention, and rehabilitation. Retributivists demand that we look backward in time, measure the blameworthiness of and harm done by an offender, and then impose the type or degree of punishment on blameworthy offenders that they deserve. Utilitarians, committed to the goal of crime prevention, argue against the reasonableness of the retributive model and urge us instead to impose punishment on blameworthy offenders only as a means of pursuing such future benefits as specific deterrence, general deterrence, marginal deterrence, and incapacitation.

Those who reject the viewpoints of both retributivists and utilitarians and who instead advocate rehabilitation ignore the relevance of blameworthiness and of harm done. Effectively, they absolve offenders of any moral responsibility for their offenses, depicting them instead as people whose criminal conduct was caused by forces they could not control (e.g., medical problems, psychological disorders, social or economic disadvantages, and so on). Those in this group thus deny that the state has a right or an obligation to punish offenders, because punishment presupposes responsible actors who have freely chosen to violate the law. They prefer to view the responses of the state as intervention strategies aimed at a very individualized treatment of the root causes of crime. Presumably such intervention strategies do require some moral justification. They do, after all, deprive people of rights and privileges they would otherwise enjoy. The apparent justification is twofold: (1) the ability of rehabilitation to modify in some positive fashion the attitudes, values, personality, skills, or behavior of those who are committed to rehabilitative programs and (2) the ability of successful rehabilitative efforts to improve the quality of life enjoyed by all citizens by decreasing or eliminating the criminal harm what would have been done by offenders had they not been rehabilitated.

You may or may not see one of these positions as being the best means of justifying our methods of dealing with those found guilty of violating the provisions of criminal law. On a theoretical level, however, you can probably see some wisdom in each. In everyday life most of us tend to believe that those who break the law deserve to be punished because of what they did in the past (a retributive sentiment), that punishment should have such future benefits as deterrence (a utilitarian goal), and that efforts to improve offenders by involving them in treatment or training programs are worthy of support (a rehabilitative objective). Indeed, a fundamental flaw in contemporary penological practice is that the appeal of retributive *and* utilitarian *and* rehabilitative perspectives has become so attractive that we have deceived ourselves into believing that we can adopt all three of these general justifications for the sentences we impose on offenders without automatically creating a host of inconsistencies and contradictions.

But the inconsistencies and the contradictions simply refuse to go away. Life would be difficult enough were we to adopt one of the three general perspectives and discard the other two. Our efforts to translate any one of them into sound and consistent legal policy and penological practice have been—to say the least—a failure. Translating the retributive model into sound sentencing policies, for instance, seems to be an entirely futile exercise simply because there is absolutely nothing in that model that permits us to define the specific punishment or range of punishment that is deserved. The fate of the utilitarian and rehabilitative perspectives continues to be equally bleak. Though these models are very different from one another in many ways, both can and must be evaluated in terms of their ability to permit us to produce what each promises—crime prevention through deterrence and incapacitation or the successful design and implementation of rehabilitative programs. Both types of promises continue to be made routinely by advocates of these two perspectives, but little or no evidence shows that either type of promise has been kept. We then compound the problems we confront by trying to pretend that rehabilitative, retributive, and utilitarian objectives can somehow be blended together and pursued within the context of what many prefer to call the American correctional system. We do so in the face of a truly awesome body of theoretical and empirical evidence which suggests that such efforts are doomed to failure before they begin.

DISCUSSION QUESTIONS

Assume that you have been chosen as the person who will write a new sentencing policy for your state, a policy that will have to be followed by each and every criminal court judge. You have been given virtually any resources you might need to accomplish this job so long as you faithfully and accurately create a sentencing policy that has a firm retributive foundation. Taking any criminal offense as your illustration, explain precisely how you determined what type or degree of punishment would be deserved by someone who intentionally engaged in that particular offense.

Now change the previous problem just a bit. Assume that the foundation would be utilitarian rather than retributive. Would that change the deserved type or degree of punishment? How? Also, how would you evaluate the extent to which your new sentencing policy achieved the future benefits you sought to achieve?

If the right of the state to intervene in the lives of its citizens and to deprive them of some of their rights, liberties, and privileges is justified by the rehabilitative potential of such an intervention, how can we continue to impose such losses on offenders when most rehabilitative efforts prove to be unsuccessful?

3

THE PAST AND PRESENT OF PENOLOGY

Criminologists seem inclined to describe the history of penology as though it revealed slow but steady progress away from exceedingly harsh, brutal, and pointless inflictions of suffering and toward more lenient, humanitarian, and sophisticated efforts to pursue the general goal of crime prevention. Perhaps there are some grains of truth in this simple summary of the evolution of punishment. At many points in history our talent for devising and routinely applying cruel methods of physical punishment has manifested itself in ways that would stagger the imagination. Still, such a historical perspective seems almost self-serving in the sense that it suggests a more or less even transition from "primitive" to "modern" cultural and legal forms.

This is a false image. Today should not be thought of as better than yesterday purely because it is today. Neither should change be viewed as progress simply because it is change. Remember, for example, that we have executed roughly 3900 offenders in the United States in the last half century or so (Bureau of Justice Statistics, 1984c). It will be only a matter of months until the death row population in this country moves above 2000. Such figures hardly suggest that our responses to crime have become altogether warm, supportive, and humanitarian.

It is also true that tracing the history of penology is made difficult for the often-ignored reason that there is relatively little of it that is of direct relevance to us today. Part of the reason for this, of course, is that punishment by its very definition involves some "lawfully imposed pain, suffering, or loss of otherwise available rights imposed on a culpable actor as a consequence of unlawful action or inaction" (Thomas and Hepburn, 1983: 544). In most practical ways the "lawfully imposed" aspect of this definition presupposes one thing regarding the nature of social organization and one thing regarding definitions of harmful actions and inactions: (1) that forms of social organization have reached the point at which something akin to the state has emerged as a power to which individual citizens and groups of citizens are subordinate; and (2) that some harmful actions and inactions have become defined as offenses against the state rather than, for example, offenses against private individuals that call for private instead of public responses.

Placed in the context of the history of Western civilization, especially the history of England, the European nation to which our system of criminal law is most indebted, the roots of a system of law and punishment even roughly similar to what we encounter today are of fairly recent vintage. (Eight centuries or so, of course, would only seem "fairly recent" to a historian!) Indeed, many centuries after complex social, political, and legal systems had developed in other parts of the world—Babylonia, Egypt, Greece, and Rome being obvious examples—Western systems remained relatively unsophisticated, lacking in terms of a centralized system of political power and given to legal provisions and remedies that today seem almost bizarre in many regards (Kempin, 1963, 1973; Ullman, 1975; Berman, 1983).

Prior to and even for a time after the Norman Conquest of England in 1066 A.D., for example, distinctions between public and private law remained crude. The law, such as it was at that point and place in history, seems to have been more oriented to creating means by which public order could be maintained by regulating private reactions to offenses than by the state itself claiming that it had been injured and thereby legitimating penal sanctions for criminal offenders. This often meant that legal resolutions of what today would be criminal matters took the form of efforts to guarantee restitution and reparation (i.e., to require that offenders compensate injured parties for their losses). Thus, under the ancient Anglo-Saxon law of England there is frequent reference to such terms as *angild,* the value of a person or an object, and *bot* and *wergild,* both terms referring to the amount of compensation an offender was required to pay to the offended party or parties (e.g., Post, 1963; Kempin, 1963, 1973; Goebel, 1976). All were used within the context of a body of law that had far more in common with provisions of contemporary private rather than public law. They reflect the state doing more to mediate conflicts between private parties than to declare some forms of misconduct as offenses committed against the state itself.

But there is more to this English and European heritage than simply who could react against whom, the form that such reactions could lawfully take, and whether the role of the state was primarily that of an independent mediator or an injured party. Post's (1963: 19) description of early English methods of ascertaining guilt and innocence illustrate the crude nature of Anglo-Saxon procedure:

Charged with crime, a man would have to submit to ordeal by fire or water or dry bread. Holding a hot iron in his hand, the accused had to walk about nine feet. According to the Laws of King Athelstan, the hand would then be bound and three days later examined by a priest. If the wound were foul, the accused was guilty; if clean, he was innocent. Or the accused might be required to plunge his arm into a pot of boiling water to retrieve a stone; again, the condition of the burn would conclude the verdict. Tied up and thrown into a stream, a man would be deemed faultless if he sank, since the pure waters had accepted him; if he rose quickly to the surface he was guilty, for the waters had rejected him; obviously either result could make him the loser. And in another ordeal, if the unfortunate accused choked on dry bread, he was pronounced guilty.

I am not contending, of course, that nothing of relevance to penological thought took place until Western societies somehow survived the rigors of the Middle Ages (roughly 500 A.D. to 1500 A.D.) and moved into the period we now refer to as the Renaissance. To advance such a claim would clearly be inaccurate. Fairly complex systems of written law, as with the Code of Hammurabi that was developed around 2250 B.C., have been with us for thousands of years. Furthermore, the view that the penal sanctions we attach to provisions of criminal law can or should do more than serve as a substitute for uncontrolled acts of revenge or as a means of compensating injured parties has a long and important history. Plato, who was born in Athens in 428 B.C., for example, used language that would not be unfamiliar today when he argued:

> No one punishes the evildoer under the notion, or for the reason, that he has done wrong—only the unreasonable fury of a beast acts in that manner. But he who desires to inflict rational punishment does not retaliate for a past wrong which cannot be undone; he has regard to the future, and is desirous that the man who is punished, and he who sees him punished, may be deterred from doing wrong again. He punishes for the sake of prevention, thereby clearly implying that virtue is capable of being taught. This is the notion of all who retaliate upon others either privately or publicly [quoted in Kittrie and Zenoff, 1981: 5].

There are, in other words, historical figures, events, and writings to which we could turn if we wished to show that the foundations of present penal practice draw on an old and respected heritage. Still other materials would support us if we wished to show that there has been a slow and steady movement away from barbarism and toward humanitarianism. Too often it seems that history (or at least historians) can be used to provide us with a means of relating the past to the present in any fashion that suits us. Perhaps that is why some critics of historical work define such work as "the selective interpretation of the past in terms of the present," or more simply as "the collective mythology of a people." Here, however, we take a simple and practical approach. We deal with penological history as though it did not really begin to unfold until sometime during the 17th century. It is for this reason that I began this section of our discussion with the observation that a portion of the difficulty in dealing with it is that there is relatively little of it.

THE ORIGINS OF REFORM IN PENAL LAW AND PRACTICE

Establishing precisely when and why the character of law—and, consequently, our methods of reacting to offenders—began to change presents us with a pair of concerns that we will not be able to resolve here. One or two things, however, seem to be both clear and important. First, both before and even for a time after the emergence of the state as the single entity that asserted that it and only it had the exclusive and legitimate right to define crimes (as opposed, for example, to what constituted unethical, immoral, or simply sinful acts), conceptions of crime and proper reactions to it tended to be shaped by a combination of the nature of the behavior in question, the relative influence, importance, and power of the offender, and the status of those who had been victimized (see, e.g., Rusche and Kirchheimer, 1939; Smith and Fried, 1974). Provisions of penal law and practice often depended as much on the particular characteristics and social status of the actors and their victims as they did on the nature or harmfulness of conduct. Consequently, early systems of law tended to include punishment provisions that considered a blending of the offense and the status of the offender as well as that of his or her victim.

The earliest written legal code, the Code of Hammurabi, contains many illustrations of this type of law (Johns, 1903). Consider the following examples:

> If a man has caused the loss of a gentleman's eye, his eye one shall cause to be lost.
> If he has shattered a gentleman's limb, one shall shatter his limb.

> If a man has made the tooth of a man that is his equal to fall out, one shall make his tooth fall out.

Now compare these provisions with others that deal with identical offenses but different status relations between victim and offender:

> If he has caused a poor man to lose his eye or shattered a poor man's limb, he shall pay one mina of silver.
> If he has caused the loss of the eye of a gentleman's servant or has shattered the limb of a gentleman's servant, he shall pay half his price.
> If he has made the tooth of a poor man to fall out, he shall pay one-third of a mina of silver.

This approach to law reveals itself time after time in legal history, and it is clearly represented in early English law (e.g., Kempin, 1963, 1973; Post, 1963; Berman, 1983). *Wergild* payments, for example, varied with the rank and status of those who were the victims of offenses.

Second, significant changes in penal law and practice came with and at least in part as a consequence of the transition from an economic and political system built upon feudalism to a system that was more compatible with what is often referred to as "mercantile capitalism" (e.g., Smith and Fried, 1974; Chambliss and Seidman, 1982; Berman, 1983). The status relationships built into early English law that defined the rights and obligations between monarchs, manorial lords, and serfs began to give way and to be shaped by the view that "public policy and law should be congruent with impersonal forces of the market place. ... Any state that interfered with these 'natural laws' of the market or the psychological propensities of man to seek his own greatest profit as a free or spontaneous creator of his own life, it was argued, had no legitimate right to govern" (Smith and Fried, 1974: 16).

The day thus passed when a major function of law was to define the rights and obligations of feudal lords to a monarch and of feudal serfs to the owners of property. The day was coming when power stemmed from successful involvement in national and international commerce and from the production of goods that could be sold at a price substantially higher than the cost paid for the labor to produce those goods. Industrial production and large-scale commerce require the sort of predictability and stability that is provided by the centralized and concentrated power of what we now refer to as the state. And the day was also coming when ever-sharper distinctions would appear between public and private law and when penal practice would begin to reflect an economic ideology that depicted all people as having an inherent ability to choose between lawful and unlawful conduct on the basis of little more than rational economic interest.

These and other preconditions for change were present well before the Colonial period of American history. Those (e.g., Mitford, 1974: 30) who have described such penal innovations as prisons as "an institution of purely American origin, conceived by its inventors as a noble humanitarian reform befitting the Age of Enlightenment" are simply incorrect (e.g., Ericksson, 1976; McKelvey, 1976). For example, the Bridewell Palace in London was converted into a prison in 1555. In 1576 Elizabeth I supported a law requiring the establishment of houses of correction in every English county. The Dutch opened the first *rasphuis,* an institution for male offenders, in 1596 and the first *spinhuis,* an institution for female offenders, soon thereafter. The St. Michael House of Correction for boys was opened in Rome in 1704 and was expanded to provide separate cells for women in 1735.

To be sure, as Eriksson (1976: 26) notes, "The various institutions all over Europe . . . were designed primarily to deal with vagrants and petty offenders who, if left to their own devices, could turn into 'real' criminals." Prisons or prisonlike facilities tended to house serious offenders only as a way of guaranteeing that they would be available for trial or to house them until they were to be punished. Typical punishments for such offenders continued to be harsh and physical (e.g., branding, enslavement, execution, and, especially with the coming of colonialism and its need for "new citizens," banishment and transportation).

Nevertheless, the seeds of change had begun to take root in Europe long before the 17th century and the colonization of this country. A new image—drawing its power from a variety of economic, political, philosophical, and religious notions—began to develop. It depicted offenders as people who could be shaped and changed and who had the ability to choose between good and evil. True, the image was fuzzy and unsophisticated, but it was there, and it was reflected in institutionally based programs aimed at, for example, instructing offenders in the moral value of discipline and physical labor as well as teaching them various vocational skills. The contention that offenders must be punished purely because of and more or less in proportion to the harm they caused began to receive less and less support. The contention that punishment could become a tool for improving future social conditions was taking form and gaining momentum.

THE BEGINNINGS OF MODERN PENOLOGY

Precisely when, where, and why the beginnings of something akin to modern penology took form are questions that are difficult if not impossible to answer with any reasonable degree of confidence. On a general level, however, the developmental sequence can be divided into two distinctively different parts. One began to take form as a consequence of a set of more or less interrelated economic, philosophical, political, and religious perspectives that became quite influential during the last quarter of the 18th century. The second materialized roughly one hundred years later. Both developments warrant at least some attention.

The Classical School of Criminology

As Europe began to move out of the Middle Ages during the 16th century and toward what we now commonly refer to as the Enlightenment, the historical record reveals only sketchy evidence of efforts aimed at dealing with convicted offenders that would approximate what we find today. Though some exceptions to this general rule have been noted already, the plight of offenders, especially those who committed what criminal law defined as serious offenses, was bleak. Much law was unwritten, and, whether written or unwritten, was biased in its content as well as its application. Secret accusations were common. The use of torture as a means of obtaining evidence and confessions had become something of an art form. Judicial decisions reflected the whims of individual judges as much or more than the rule of law. And methods of punishment, to say the very least, were brutal. Consider the following summary provided by Maestro (1973: 13-15, emphasis in original):

> The death penalty and bodily mutilations, rather than prison terms, were the usual punishments for the majority of crimes. For minor offenses the most frequent penalties were flogging and such corporal mutilations as slitting or piercing the tongue, and cutting or burning off the hand. For offenses such as perjury or bribery the customary penalty was the pillory; these devices were set up in public places, and the pains of exposure were increased by the jeers and insults of the onlookers. In Rome the pillories were erected on the Capitoline steps, and Cantu relates that the faces of the culprits were daubed with honey so they would attract flies. ... Capital punishments were of various kinds: burning at the stake was the regular punishment for heresy, while for other crimes the most unusual forms of execution were hanging, quartering, and breaking on the wheel. ... Hanging was the regular form of execu-

tion [in England], but a worse penalty was reserved for a man guilty of high treason: in accordance with an old custom he was dragged along the ground at the tail of a horse, with only a grate to protect his head from knocking on the stones; then he was hanged and from his still living body the entrails were pulled out and thrown into the fire; after that his head was cut off and the body quartered. In the eighteenth century this custom was somewhat softened: the entrails were pulled out *after* the condemned man had ceased to breathe.

Resistance to such a harsh and oppressive system of justice was apparent in this country even during the Colonial period. William Penn, a Quaker who became the first governor of Pennsylvania in 1681, for example, is often cited as an early reformer whose religious convictions encouraged him to lobby for a milder and more humane set of reactions to offenders. McKelvey (1976: 3) identifies Penn as "the first responsible leader to prescribe imprisonment as a corrective treatment for major offenders."

Practically speaking, however, it was not until almost one hundred years later and with the emergence of the Classical School of criminology that punishments like fines and terms of imprisonment became accepted as a reasonable substitute for corporal punishment and executions. This notion, advanced in some preliminary ways by such philosophers of the period as Montesquieu (1689-1755), Voltaire (1694-1778), and Rousseau (1712-1778), began to attract broad public and political support following the publication of Beccaria's (1738-1794) exceedingly influential *On Crimes and Punishments* in 1764 and the works of such later utilitarian writers as Bentham (1748-1832).

The basic position advanced by utilitarian philosophers and social reformers such as Beccaria and Bentham was reviewed in Chapter 2, so we need not retrace all of that ground here. The proper purpose of law, they argued, "is to augment the total happiness of the community; and therefore, in the first place, to exclude, as far as may be, everything that tends to subtract from that happiness: in other words, to exclude mischief" (Bentham, 1975: 25). Punishment, of course, deserved to be viewed as a "mischief" that was to be avoided—unless it had the ability to prevent some even greater mischief. Thus, they concluded, punishment was to be avoided if it lacked the ability to serve its preventive purposes, if the harm caused by offenses proved to be less than the harm caused by punishment itself, or if some alternative to punishment would serve preventive goals equally well. Punishment could be justified under many other circumstances, however. For example, Bentham (1975: 28) identified the most important purposes of punishment as including the following: (1) the prevention of all offenses, (2) the prevention of the most harmful offenses (i.e., convincing offenders who could not be persuaded to avoid crime altogether to at least choose from less harmful types of offenses), and (3) the minimization of harm done by offenses that cannot be prevented. Pursuing these future benefits of punishment was to be done by selecting the minimum possible punishment required.

The most significant means by which Beccaria, Bentham, and their counterparts hoped to prevent crime are well known and were reviewed in Chapter 2. They recommended that legislation and the application of law seek to manipulate three primary elements of punishment: the certainty of punishment, the swiftness of punishment, and the severity of punishment. Fully aware of the difficulties involved in manipulating these properties of punishment, the utilitarians argued that shortcomings in one or more areas could be compensated for by actions taken in other areas. Recall, for example, Bentham's (1975: 30) assertion: "To enable the value of punishment to outweigh that of the profit of the offence, it must be increased, in point of magnitude, in proportion as it falls short in point of certainty....Punishment must be further increased in point of magnitude, in proportion as it falls short in point of proximity."

Four major influences were thus coming together as we moved into the closing decades of the 18th century. First, Western societies had moved away from an economic system based on the maintenance of special legal and social relationships between landowners and those who worked the lands and toward a more complex system within which large-scale commerce and the production of goods were becoming increasingly important. Second, as the power of centralized political entities increased, crimes came to be defined as offenses against the state rather than against individual persons. Third, religious ideologies were coming to assign more significance to the possiblity that reactions to offenders could serve the goal of reform as well as retribution. Fourth, the works of the utilitarian philosophers associated with the Classical School of criminology were popularizing the view that humans are endowed with the capacity to engage in rational thought and are free to choose between good and evil on the basis of their perceptions of which choice will yield the greater benefits at the lower cost.

The Birth of the Penitentiary

The beginnings of modern penology were established during the closing decades of the 18th century. The punishment provisions of criminal law came to be viewed as an opportunity for a great humanitarian leap forward that had the power to simultaneously eliminate the arbitrary and discriminatory application of law, lessen if not eliminate the need to rely on corporal and capital punishment, provide a context within which offenders could appreciate the need to reform themselves, and provide an effective means for achieving such objectives as deterrence and incapacitation. A major vehicle for all of this was to be the penitentiary. The immediate problem was to determine the precise type of prison within which all of these lofty purposes could best be achieved.

The "Pennsylvania System" versus the "Auburn System"

Two basic models for prisons were advanced as terms of confinement for serious offenders began to be seen as appropriate alternatives to such traditional sentences as flogging, branding, and execution. One, the *Pennsylvania System*, originated in large part from the reform efforts of the Philadelphia Society for Alleviating the Miseries of Public Prisons, a group formed in 1787. The group was instrumental in lobbying that resulted in changes in the Pennsylvania penal code and expansion of the facilities of the Walnut Street Jail in Philadelphia on which construction had begun in 1773. The penal philosophy they advanced was fairly simple. Serious offenders, they felt, could best be reformed if they were kept in strict isolation and sentenced to terms of hard labor. Less serious offenders would also be required to work, but they would not need to be so carefully isolated from one another. A small cell block containing a total of 16 cells intended for those offenders who were to be kept in solitary confinement was completed in 1792.

You can easily imagine the difficulties one would encounter, the costs one would have to assume, and the potential damage one might do to offenders if one were to create a system that effectively isolated offenders from one another for a protracted period of time. Nevertheless, the zeal of those who were convinced that solitary confinement at hard labor was the road to reformation and salvation of offenders, a road that would "instead of continuing habits of vice, become the means of restoring our fellow creatures to virtue and happiness" (quoted in McKelvey, 1976: 7), was considerable. Western Penitentiary, for example, was constructed near Pittsburg in 1826 and included 190 cells that were designed in a fashion—even though it proved to be unsuccessful—intended to provide for the total isolation of each inmate. Pennsylvania opened still another of this type of penitentiary, Eastern Penitentiary (though it is most often referred to as Cherry Hill), in 1830. This innovation later proved attractive elsewhere in the United States (e.g., New Jersey) and in many European nations (e.g., England, France, Holland, and Sweden; Barnes, 1968).

The alternative to the Pennsylvania System was the *Auburn System,* which some say began with the opening of Newgate Prison in New York during the last decade of the 18th century and which attracted significant international attention when Auburn Prison popularized it in the early 1820s. Officials at Auburn initially had experimented with the solitary confinement methods characteristic of the Pennsylvania System but had found them to be largely counterproductive. Kept in nearly total isolation with little or no work to occupy them and equally scant opportunity for exercise or other diversions, inmates were pushed beyond the limits of psychological endurance. William Brittin, Auburn's designer and first warden, died in 1821 and was replaced by Elam Lynds; soon after, a quest for a more viable set of practices was underway. The plan called for inmates to work together in complete silence in carefully supervised workshops during the daytime and to be isolated from one another in individual cells during the evening hours. Discipline was strict and harsh, with violations of prison rules meeting swift punishment (for more detailed discussion and description, see Lewis, 1965; Barnes, 1968; Eriksson, 1976; McKelvey, 1976).

Suffice it to say that support for the Pennsylvania System in this country soon withered away and that the only modestly softer practices associated with the Auburn System—which is to say large prisons within which inmates were most commonly confined in single-person cells at night but forced to engage in congregate labor projects during daytime hours—became the model for American penology. Indeed, many of the prisons constructed during the 1800s under the influence of the philosophy of the Auburn System remain in use today. This result, depending largely on one's point of view, can be thought of either positively or negatively. On the positive side, of course, the movement away from physically harsh and often brutal punishment and toward more humane—even if only modestly more humane—reactions to offenders is evaluated quite positively by most penologists. So, too, are those features of the Auburn System that abolished the long periods of nearly total isolation in solitary confinement recommended by advocates of the Pennsylvania System. On the negative side, however, the rigidity of the Auburn System and its lack of more than the most rudimentary ideas about either the causes of crime or the means by which it could best be prevented hardly elevated it to a position that warrants thinking of it as a sophisticated step in the evolution of penal practice.

The Emergence of the Rehabilitative Ideal

Well before the Civil War began in the United States, prisons had become an accepted feature of the penological landscape. Punishment motivated primarily by a desire for vengeance or by a commitment to retributive principles had been displaced at least in part by a conviction that properly administered punishment could serve the goal of crime prevention through deterrence, incapacitation, and reformation. In many ways, however, penological practice had little to direct it beyond a general notion that those who chose to commit crimes could be persuaded to refrain from such harmful conduct if they experienced the various deprivations of imprisonment. The winds of change, however, were once again preparing to drive penology into a new era. What is now referred to as the *rehabilitative ideal* was about to make its presence felt.

Just as we found it difficult to identify the precise point at which modern penology began to take form and were more or less forced to identify the turning point as having been provided by such Classical School criminologists as Beccaria and Bentham, identifying when where, and at the urging of whom the rehabilitative ideal emerged may be an impossible task. As was noted in Chapter 2, however, a firm belief that crime is not a product of free choices made by rational actors is at the very core of the rehabilitative approach. Instead we find the conviction that offenders are driven to crime by forces over which they have little or no personal control and the obvious implication that crime prevention requires that we tinker in some way with those root causes of crime rather than seeking to punish individual offenders.

It must be emphasized that the emergence of the rehabilitative ideal and the development of causal theories of crime which view it as being caused by factors other than rational choice did not take place at the same time in history. Quetelet and many other European criminologists, for example, had become involved in fairly sophisticated empirical research on the causes of crime early in the 19th century. Many point to the "Statistical School" or "Ecological School" with which they were associated as marking the early beginnings of criminology as a scientific field of inquiry (e.g., Thomas and Hepburn, 1983: 120-163). In contrast, support for a rehabilitative emphasis in penology did not begin to take form until the last quarter of the 19th century, with the development of what is most commonly referred to today as the *Positive School* of criminology.

We need not labor over the sometimes bizarre and usually misleading works of such representatives of the Positive School at Lombroso (but see, for example, Lombroso, 1968; Lombroso-Ferrero, 1972; Vold and Bernard, 1979: 35-48; Thomas and Hepburn, 1983: 146-158). At the heart of this body of work, however, is the conviction that offenders are essentially driven to crime by a set of biological, psychological, and environmental factors that can be identified by systematic scientific research. Crime, therefore, was said to be something substantially similar to a symptom of an underlying disease, defect, or disorder. Thus, proper reactions to crime were said to demand careful diagnosis and individualized treatment rather than efforts to punish in accordance with the logic of either retributive or utilitarian perspectives on punishment.

The foundations for a penological theory that was to dominate much penal law and practice until (and perhaps including) today can be easily I think accurately traced back to this single development in the history of criminology. Much of the needed apparatus to translate rehabilitative perspectives into actual practice had slowly accumulated over a period of hundreds of years. With the centralization of political power that came with the modern state, the view that crime was to be an object of public rather than private law (i.e., that crimes were really offenses against the state rather than individual victims) had become a dominant feature of substantive criminal law. The reform efforts of the utilitarian philosophers associated with the Classical School of criminology had marked a major movement away from a routine reliance on corporal and capital punishment and toward the presumably more humanitarian alternative of confinement. These reformers, however, had relatively little to say about precisely how prisons could go about the difficult business of preventing crime (though some, especially Bentham, did become sufficiently involved in the practical aspects of penology and labored over detailed designs for the "ideal prison").

As penologists moved toward the 20th century, many were convinced that they had "seen the light" and that they could soon devise a blueprint for success. Gone, they concluded, were the days when punishment should be imposed in an effort to guarantee that offenders would receive their "just deserts" in accordance with the retributive philosophy of sentencing. Gone, too, were the days when punishment should be imposed in the hope that doing so would produce such future benefits as those emphasized by the utilitarians. Emerging was the day when we would view offenders as persons driven to criminal conduct, as persons who deserved to be viewed by the state as individuals whose harmful conduct pointed to the need for efficient, effective, and highly individualized treatment.

For serious offenders, an important context within which rehabilitative efforts could be pursued was to be the prison. However, those committed to prison would not receive the sort of fixed and rigid sentences advocated—though for very different reasons—by both the retributivists and the utilitarians. Instead, argued those advocating the rehabilitative perspective, individual cases should come before the courts purely in an effort to distinguish between the innocent and the guilty. Those found guilty should receive either a largely indeterminate sentence (e.g., a prison term of from 1 to 15 years) or a totally indeterminate sentence (e.g., a prison term running potentially from the point of sentencing to life imprisonment). "Correctional experts" would then produce a proper diagnosis, prepare an appropriate treatment plan, and retain the full power to release offenders whenever they determined that a rehabilitative success had been produced.

Paving the Road to Hell with Good Intentions

Our quick trip through several hundred years of developments in penological theory and practice is now complete, but it would be a mistake to move further without first injecting one exceedingly important qualification. Specifically, any effort to divide penological history into rough phases of its development can easily leave the impression that the appeal of one phase withered away as the zeal with which a subsequent phase was adopted began to grow. Earlier sections of this chapter, for instance, could be interpreted to mean that the attractiveness of the deterrence doctrine advanced by those associated with the classical school of criminology was replaced by enthusiasm for the "disease model" of the Positive School and its advocacy of a rehabilitative approach.

Carefully avoid any inclination you might have to interpret what has been said in so simple a fashion. The field of penology has demonstrated all of the proclivities we commonly associate with the proverbial pack rat: It almost never throws anything away. This is true even with regard to such presumably "primitive" punishments as branding, mutilation, and other methods of responding to offenders that some thought had disappeared during the Middle Ages. Consider, for example, contemporary recommendations that rapists be castrated or that brain surgery and electric shock "therapy" be used to pacify various forms of offenders. Consider, too, our great public and legal fondness for executing offenders—a fondness that has resulted in something on the order of 10,000 executions during the past 100 years —in the total absence of reliable scientific evidence that executions serve any goal of punishment as well as or better than a variety of less severe sanctions (e.g., life imprisonment without opportunity for parole).

The point is not simply that the veneer of civilization is so very thin that our lust for "blood and gore" persists—though I think that such an observation would be entirely valid. The real point is that we have a remarkable ability to add more and more goals to the list of what correctional practitioners are asked to achieve while somehow remaining in a state of blissful ignorance regarding the frequency with which those goals flatly and obviously contradict one another. Some become convinced that the logic of a retributive position is quite attractive. As a result, that becomes a goal of our penal system. Some become convinced that the logic of a utilitarian position is quite attractive, and that becomes a goal of our penal system. Some become convinced that the logic of a rehabilitative position is quite attractive, and it too becomes a goal of our penal system. But can anyone reasonably and rationally expect the same penal system to pursue with equal fervor the goals of retribution, deterrence, and rehabilitation? Can anyone expect it to somehow prioritize these general goals by giving, for example, primary attention to the retributive and deterrence objectives and secondary attention to rehabilitation?

The answers to these questions should be obvious enough to anyone who has read this and the previous chapter. The logical and operational problems we would encounter if we were to seriously pursue any one perspective on penology would be acute. The predictable outcome of any effort to "mix and match" such contradictory points of view is almost certain to be confusion and abject failure. Our failure to recognize this reality is one of the major reasons for the common feeling that the prospects for our penal system are bleak. We have reached no agreement about the objectives the system should be trying to achieve. Instead, we demand that it pursue a host of contradictory objectives. To ask correctional practitioners, in effect, to chase their own tails seems awfully foolish. To make a national pastime out of criticizing them when they fail to do the impossible can hardly be taken as a demonstration of our collective brilliance.

CONTEMPORARY CORRECTIONS IN AMERICA

We soon turn our attention to some of the more significant problems and controversies that are attracting the interest of both academic penologists and correctional practitioners. Before doing so, however, some image of contemporary efforts in the field must be created. This must be done, whether fortunately or unfortunately, without consuming too much time or space. I admit to being at something of a loss regarding how this can best be accomplished, especially when I think of how easily readers brush statistical information aside.

This reservation notwithstanding, in what follows I have done my best to select figures in an effort to make several points. First, to understand many of the problems confronting correctional practitioners today, and perhaps also to understand why we continue to see such bleak results when correctional efforts are evaluated objectively, one must first achieve a general appreciation for the sheer volume of criminal behavior that occurs within our society and the highly selective process that determines, in effect, one's eligibility for involvement in correctional programs. Second, it is important to gain some insight regarding the nature of the sentencing process, which stands as the final step in a multistage process that begins with a criminal act and that can—but seldom does—result in the state imposing a sentence on a convicted offender. Finally, attention must be given to the magnitude as well as the social and demographic characteristics of the population of persons presently under correctional supervision of one type or another, and to the resource base on which correctional practitioners can depend as they attempt to achieve their various objectives.

Crime and Victimization in the United States

Much public and professional attention has been devoted to information about the amount of crime in the United States. We are bombarded with such data on almost a daily basis. Rates of crimes against persons and/or property are said to be going up, down, or remaining under control. This information, in turn, is used by everyone who has even a passing interest in the problem of crime—private citizens, law enforcement officials, politicians, and so on—to prove just about anything that someone seeks to prove. Indeed, the same statistics are routinely used by opposing groups to demonstrate, for example, that crime is both under and out of control, that police need both more and fewer resources, that the courts are doing both a sound and a horrible job, and that correctional practitioners are both achieving and not even getting close to the goals they have been assigned to pursue.

In some ways these kinds of obvious contradictions reflect little more than very different points of view. Just as beauty is said to be in the eye of the beholder, so the "true meaning" of crime statistics is likely to be found in the personal, economic, and political interests of those who claim some ability to interpret them. The contradictions also provide a good illustration of the skeptical position that is summarized by the saying, "Figures don't lie, but all liars figure."

But there is more to the present dilemma than various interests determining interpretations and self-serving manipulations of statistical information. Much of this situation is closely linked to one very simple fact: *At the present time we have no acceptably reliable and valid means by which we can go about the business of measuring the incidence of the harm caused by crime in this or any other nation.* About the only thing that we can say with any reasonable confidence comes in two parts: (1) there is a tremendous amount of crime taking place "out there"—crime that causes substantial harm in terms of economic, physical, and psychological costs to those who are victimized—and (2) a difficult to estimate but large proportion of the total volume of crime escapes being included in our statistical database for the simple reason that victims of offenses do not report having been victimized to those who collect that statistical information.

These two fairly vague summary statements require some elaboration. To begin with, for a long time our only national source of information about the incidence of crime in the United States was provided by reports prepared by an agency of the federal government, the Federal Bureau of Investigation. Since 1930 the FBI has collected information regarding a variety of things—especially "crimes known to the police" and "crimes cleared by arrest"—from thousands (more than 15,000 last year) of law enforcement agencies serving communities throughout the United States. Summaries of these data are issued by the FBI in an abbreviated manner on a quarterly basis and in a far more detailed manner on an annual basis. The "crimes known" portion of these data describes the number of various types of crimes that have been reported to the police (primarily by private citizens and business concerns that have been victimized). The "crimes cleared" data provide a crude measure of the efficiency and effectiveness of law enforcement agencies as they go about the task of apprehending persons who are believed to be responsible for reported crimes (e.g., the percentage of the known homicide offenses during a given year that resulted in the arrest—though not necessarily the prosecution or conviction—of a suspect).

Presumably in an effort to simplify life for those who use the *Uniform Crime Reports,* the annual document published by the FBI, the data on reported crimes are routinely divided into two parts: *Part I,* or *Crime Index Offenses,* and *Part II.* The former category is said to include especially serious felony offenses (e.g., criminal homicide, assault, rape, armed robbery, larceny-theft, auto theft, burglary, and arson); the latter category includes virtually all other criminal offenses as well as some offenses for which only juveniles may be prosecuted (e.g., running away from home). Despite the narrow scope of the category, the vast majority of attention focuses on the Crime Index offenses. This set of offenses is used—very wrongly and with an array of conservative political implications that are beyond the scope of this discussion—as though data about them provided a representative sample of information about the overall problem of crime in the United States. Flaws and limitations aside, these data clearly show that crime is a very serious social and legal problem. Based on the volume of reported Crime Index offenses in recent years, there is ample reason to believe that roughly 14 million such offenses will be brought to the attention of law enforcement agencies this year (e.g., Brown et al., 1984: 370).

As large as these estimates of the incidence of crime are, they grossly underestimate the true dimensions of the crime problem that provides the "raw material" for those who hold positions as correctional practitioners. Part of the problem, of course, is that a huge number of crimes fall beyond the boundaries of the Crime Index Offense category. Their number and the harm they cause may or may not be so highly correlated with the Crime Index Offenses that knowledge about increases or decreases in the volume of Crime Index offenses tells us something about the fluctuations in the number of other types of offenses. Equally if not more important, however, is the fact that an exceedingly large number of criminal offenses are never brought to the attention of law enforcement agencies. Recent survey data, for instance, provide a basis for estimating that 23.62 million of the 86.15 million households in the United States experienced a criminal victimization during 1983 (Bureau of Justice Statistics, 1984a). In other words, during the period of a single year, more than 27 percent of all the households in the nation had a direct experience with one or more crimes against property and/or person.

Related research on the frequency with which criminal victimizations remain unreported pushes the defects in official crime statistics into sharp relief. For example, a large survey conducted during 1982 as part of a major governmental effort to estimate the size of the "hidden figure of crime" resulted in lengthy interviews with members of some 60,000 households (Bureau of Justice Statistics, 1984b). Members of these households were asked to report on their experiences as the victims of criminal offenses during 1982 and to indicate whether they had or had not reported such victimizations to the police. Of those who had been victimized during the year, less than half made reports to the police. Specifically, only 26.9 percent of all theft offenses and 48.2 percent of all crimes against persons had been reported to the police (Bureau of Justice Statistics, 1984b: 71). To be sure, many of these victimizations involved relatively nonserious crimes that caused little or no personal or economic loss. This is perhaps the primary reason why 26.1 percent of those not reporting victimizations indicated that they failed to do so because they thought it was not sufficiently important (Bureau of Justice Statistics, 1984b: 75). However, large fractions of serious offenses also remained unreported. To cite but a few illustrations, 45.3 percent of rapes, 41.5 percent of robberies, 51.3 percent of assaults, and 49.4 percent of burglaries remained unreported (Bureau of Justice Statistics, 1984b: 70).

The Criminal Justice Process

We need not pursue the related issues of reported and unreported crime any further here. It is abundantly clear that the magnitude of the crime problem confronting those working in the various components of our criminal justice system is huge. It must be recognized, however, that our correctional system encounters only those who move through the multistage criminal justice system to the point at which a criminal court judge sentences them to some term and type of correctional supervision. Their offenses must become known to the authorities. They must be found and arrested. Prosecutors must file charges against them and take their cases before a criminal court. They must then be found guilty and either deserving of or in need of what a given correctional system has to offer.

Speaking in purely practical terms, if the correctional system were called upon to deal with more than a small fraction of the total offender population, the demands placed on that system would be so much greater than the available resource base that the system would be destroyed almost immediately. But that theoretical possibility causes little concern among correctional practitioners. They know all too well that the "front end" of the criminal justice system is so remarkably inefficient as its representatives go about the business of detecting, apprehending, and prosecuting offenders that only a tiny fraction will ever see the inside of a courtroom.

Consider, to begin with, the fact that year in and year out, the police will be able to arrest a suspect in roughly 20 percent of all the cases that are classified as Crime Index offenses (and remember that many if not most of these especially serious felonies are never even reported to the police). In one reporting period, for example, arrests took place in 72 percent of the reported criminal homicide cases, 58 percent of aggravated assaults, 48 percent of rapes, 24 percent of robberies, 19 percent of larceny-thefts, 14 percent of burglaries, and 14 percent of auto thefts (Bureau of Justice Statistics, 1983: 52). Because crimes against property are far more common than crimes against persons, the overall percentage of these Crime Index offenses that resulted in an arrest during the same reporting period was 19 percent. (On the other hand, keep in mind that a low percentage of offenses cleared by arrests can still produce a large number of arrests when the volume of reported crime is as high as it is in the United States. The 19 percent clearance rate just described, for example, produced 2,420,000 arrests for Crime Index offenses and 8,419,200 arrests for other non-Index offenses—or 10,840,000 arrests during a single calendar year.)

What we see, then, is that (1) the likelihood of an arrest following most types of criminal acts is far lower than most people would imagine but that (2) the number of suspects who are arrested during a typical year creates a tremendous pool of potential "correctional clients." Most of those arrested, however, "bounce off" the system at some point before the need arises to impose any type of sentence. The reasons for case attrition are numerous. Evidence is deemed to be insufficient to support a successful prosecution or, if sufficient, was obtained in a manner that precludes its use in court (e.g., improper warrantless searches). Prosecutors decide that cases are not important enough to deserve their attention. Witnesses or victims refuse to testify. It is determined that defendants are juveniles who either cannot or should not be prosecuted in criminal courts. The list goes on and on, and it certainly must include decisions to prosecute or refuse to prosecute that stem from the social, economic, and political power of both victims and defendants (e.g., Black, 1970, 1976; Carroll and Mondrick, 1976; Thomas and Fitch, 1977; Petersilia, 1983). The effect, however, is dramatic.

Consider the following illustration provided by research on the movement of cases through the criminal justice process in Washington, D. C., that was completed as part of a much larger study. Of each typical set of 100 felony cases that came to the attention of Washington prosecutors, 17 were rejected when they were evaluated initially, and 34 were dropped out of the system after prosecutors filed charges only to change their minds later. This left 49 cases that the prosecutors wished to bring into a criminal court. As is common in our system of bargained justice, 42 of the 49 resulted in defendants entering a plea of guilty (Rosett and Cressey, 1976; Eisenstein and Jacobs, 1977; Heumann, 1978; Zeisel, 1981; Bureau of Justice Statistics, 1984d; Farr, 1984). The remaining seven of each typical set of 100 felony cases demanded a trial. Of these, guilty verdicts were obtained in five and acquittals were the consequence in two. Naturally, case dispositions will vary with any number of variables—time period under consideration, locality, type of offense, background of defendants, quality of evidence obtained, public and political pressure applied to representatives of the criminal justice system, and so on—but the Washington figures are certainly not atypical.

The picture should now be coming into focus. While we have not yet reached the point in the criminal justice process at which sentences are to be imposed, the number of cases that have dropped out of or simply never got into the criminal justice system for one reason or another is exceedingly large. Say, for instance, that we were following 100 "garden variety" felony offenses from the point of those offenses having taken place only up to the point at which defendants were to be placed on trial. How many of the 100 offenders would we be dealing with when our set of hypothetical trials began? Crudely calculated, it would appear to shake down in the following fashion. Fifty would be no problem at all because the victims of their criminal conduct would fail to make any report to the police (e.g., Bureau of Justice Statistics, 1984b). Because arrests take place in only about 20 percent of reported Crime Index offenses, roughly ten of the remaining 50 cases would result in the arrest of a suspect (e.g., Bureau of Justice Statistics, 1984d: 52). Roughly five of these ten cases would drop out of the system before any trial began because of decisions made by prosecutors. Thus, only some 5 percent of those who commit felony offenses in the United States today seem likely to confront the risk of appearing before a criminal court as a consequence of their unlawful acts. This is hardly the sort of outcome imagined by the criminologists associated with the Classical School of criminology when they spoke in terms of our ability to deter crime through swift, certain, and adequately severe punishment!

Despite the massive number of cases that fall through one of the many cracks in the criminal justice system prior to trial, the burden placed on our criminal courts—and subsequently on our correctional system—is still excessive given the resources that have been made available to them. In 1981, for example, our criminal courts confronted more than 12 million filings of misdemeanor and felony actions against adult defendants and substantially more than 1 million actions filed against juveniles (Brown et al., 1984: 474-495). It is reasonable to estimate that roughly 70 percent of the cases coming before our criminal courts result in defendants being convicted and sentenced (Brosi, 1979; Brown et al., 1984: 507).

The Narrow End of the Criminal Justice Funnel

The Size and Characteristics of the "Client" Population

Despite the tediousness of all these summary statistics, we need to push a bit further before we close this chapter by looking at the number and characteristics of those who reach the end of the criminal justice "funnel" and at the resource base available to the correctional system they encounter when they are sentenced. The volume aspect of the discussion can be summarized quite simply. Recent figures released by various governmental agencies show that state and federal correctional systems are responsible for supervising approximately 1.5 million probationers, 250,000 parolees, 225,000 persons held in local jail facilities, 500,000 adult inmates confined in state or federal prisons, and 50,000 juveniles housed in public detention, correctional, and shelter facilities (Office of Juvenile Justice and Delinquency Prevention, 1983; Bureau of Justice Statistics, 1984e, 1984f, 1985a). Today, therefore, the total population under some type of correctional supervision is estimated to be something in excess of 2.5 million persons.

Though fairly accurate materials are available regarding the gross number of offenders who are under one or another form of correctional supervision, it is remarkable that so little is reported regarding the social, legal, and demographic characteristics of those persons. Some of this paucity of data can be explained by, for example, the fact that around half of those confined in jail are persons who have not yet been convicted on any criminal charge (Bureau of Justice Statistics, 1984e: 6), the relatively nonserious offenses committed by many probationers and a significant number of confined juvenile delinquents (e.g., Office of Juvenile Justice and Delinquency Prevention, 1983), and the very large number of persons who both come under and are released from correctional supervision each year (Brown et al., 1984). Still, one would expect far more detailed and routinely reported data regarding those offenders who have been committed to a term of imprisonment in a state or federal prison. Such data are unavailable in a suitably current form as this is being written.

The shortcomings of data notwithstanding, a general profile of those offenders deemed to be serious enough to warrant commitment to a state or federal prison would look something like the following. First, the offender is most likely to be a male (only about 4.5 percent of inmates are female; Bureau of Justice Statistics, 1985a). Second, the offender is almost equally likely to be nonwhite or white. One breakdown on the ethnic/racial profile of prison inmates, for example, showed that 51.3 percent were white, 46.8 percent were black, and the race/ethnicity of the remainder was either something else or unknown (Bureau of Justice Statistics, 1980: 18). Third, the typical inmate is a good deal younger than the typical person in the general population (e.g., more than half of all inmates are between the ages of 20 and 29, but less than one-third of the general population falls into this age range; U.S. Department of Justice, 1979: 5-6). Less than half of the inmate population, as opposed to nearly three-quarters of the general population, has completed a high school education, and one-third or more report having had neither a full- nor a part-time job during the period just before they were arrested (U.S. Department of Justice, 1979; Bureau of Justice Statistics, 1982). A majority of those who were employed held positions that we would classify as unskilled or semiskilled.

In short, the typical offender sentenced to a term in prison tends to be a young, poorly educated male—quite often a member of a minority group—whose access to meaningful vocational opportunities is seriously limited by, among other things, his lack of marketable skills. Beyond those general background characteristics, he is likely to have committed a serious felony against either a person (roughly 52 percent of the confined population) or property (another 33 percent of the population), though a significant number were confined after convictions on drug charges of one kind or another (10 percent of the population; U.S. Department of Justice, 1979: 2). He is thus likely to have an average sentence of 8.63 years. This sentence is commonly shortened significantly by provisions for "time off for good behavior," early release on parole, or other means of lessening time actually spent in prison (Bureau of Justice Statistics, 1982: 2). Finally, the typical offender is unlikely to confront a new experience when he enters prison. Recent reports, for instance, suggest that more than 60 percent of newly committed offenders have prior records of confinement and that a similarly high percentage of those with no prior record of confinement did have a prior record of convictions that had resulted in their being placed on probation (Bureau of Justice Statistics, 1985b).

The Resource Base of the Correctional System

Regardless of whether you view the proper objective of our penal system as being primarily one of just punishment, crime prevention through deterrence and incapacitation, or rehabilitation, you have to admit that no goal or combination of goals can be pursued cheaply. A fact of contemporary life is that you get what you pay for—and then only if you're lucky. Unfortunately for all of us—more or less law-abiding citizens and offenders alike—neither we nor the politicians who pretend to represent us seem to realize that this fact of life applies to what is to be done within our penal system. It is thus tempting to summarize the resource base for the system by saying that it amounts to little more than a joke—a bad joke.

This sort of joke warrants at least a general definition that provides some quantitative data. Creating such data requires a bit of speculative effort in the sense that much of the available information has become dated (e.g., Bureau of Justice Statistics, 1981), but a combination of older and some newer data (e.g., Bureau of Justice Statistics, 1985a) provides a basis for some general estimates. The "best guess" speculation for the general resource base of corrections has the following parameters. First of all, based on an estimated expenditure of some $31.27 billion for all operations of all components of the criminal justice system in 1984 and a historical "corrections share" of total expenditures of around 23 percent, our state and federal correctional systems—including programs aimed at juvenile offenders—had access to something in the neighborhood of $7.55 billion last year (Bureau of Justice Statistics, 1985a: 5). Past experience suggests that approximately 60 percent of these dollars were allocated to state correctional systems, 35 percent to local systems, and 5 percent to federal programs and facilities. Though a significant fraction of these funds were devoted to the capital outlays for the construction or modification of new facilities—state and federal prison systems, for example, added space for 67,000 more inmates between 1981 and 1983 at an average cost per added space of more than $30,000—the vast majority of the correctional budget went to cover the costs associated with the more than 200,000 full-time employees working within the correctional system in one capacity or another (e.g., probation officers, parole officers, prison employees, and so on; Bureau of Justice Statistics, 1981: 33, 1983: 93, 1985a).

Examined in isolation from any point of comparison, the resource base for our correctional systems may seem to be considerable. Billions of dollars per year in allocations hardly fall into the range of small change. At the same time, this expenditure has been estimated to require a per capita investment of a fairly modest $28.00 per year. Total state and local government expenditures reached $1911 per capita per year in 1980 (Bureau of Justice Statistics, 1983: 100)—not to mention the fact that interest payments on our national debt have been estimated to cost each taxpayer in the nation approximately $500 per year. Corrections, then, is hardly a "big ticket item" when its costs are placed into a comparative perspective.

The results of our asking too few to accomplish too much with too little have created something close to a national disgrace. By the end of this year we may well have close to 3 million offenders under some form of correctional supervision. Many of them will be housed in one of our 3500 or so local jails or in our federal and state prisons, which will soon number 600 or more (Bureau of Justice Statistics, 1983: 78-79). The typical prison facility is now operating at significantly above its maximum population capacity—some, including Hawaii, Indiana, Massachusetts, Ohio, and Oregon, are operating with inmate populations 30 percent or more above the maximum (Bureau of Justice Statistics, 1985a: 7). Indeed, prison conditions have become so offensive in so many areas that one state system after another is finding that both federal and state courts are more than willing to declare portions if not all of their prison operations to be flatly unconstitutional. During 1984, 11,555 offenders sentenced to prison terms had to be housed in local jails rather than state prisons, and another 17,365 inmates were given early releases from state prisons purely because suitable space to house them simply did not exist (Bureau of Justice Statistics, 1985a: 5-7). Substantially the same plight confronts those under probation or parole supervision and those committed to various types of noninstitutionally based correctional programs. It is not uncommon, for example, for a single probation or parole officer to confront a caseload of 100-150 offenders and to then be asked to monitor them very closely throughout the term of their probation or parole supervision. It is, of course, a frustrating and entirely impossible task.

SUMMARY

A thorough assessment of the history and evolution of punishment would require us to go back to the earliest beginnings of human experience. For example, formal systems of written law, as with the Code of Hammurabi, began to develop some 4000 years ago. Those early bodies of law, which included detailed descriptions of the types and degrees of punishment that were to be imposed on offenders, were later to influence the development of Greek, Roman, and many other ancient bodies of law. All of this took place well before the governmental and legal institutions of most of Europe began to emerge in anything remotely akin to their modern form. Nevertheless, a reasonable understanding of penal philosophy and practice in the United States can be achieved by looking back to the experience of Western European nations—especially England—from roughly the time of the Norman Conquest in 1066. During the next few centuries the English monarchs were able to establish themselves as the heads of an increasingly powerful and centralized state. Criminal offenses soon came to be defined as offenses against the state—in other words, a problem to be dealt with by public law—rather than as harm caused by one individual who therefore should be required to compensate his or her victim in one fashion or another.

As the political, religious, economic, and legal institutions of English society began to change and become increasingly more complex, the methods of and rationale for punishing offenders also changed dramatically. By no later than the 16th century, for example, there is evidence of some exploratory efforts aimed at relying on punishments other than branding, banishment, executions, and other types of harsh sanctions that were commonplace during that phase of legal history. The first really major transformation of penal law and practice, however, did not find broad popular and political support until the rise of the Classical School of criminology in the late 1700s. The utilitarian perspective that so thoroughly dominated classical thought depicted all of us as being rational actors who, being primarily motivated by our own self-interest, could be drawn away from unlawful conduct by a combination of adequately swift, certain, and severe punishments. These reactions, reasoned members of the Classical School, could serve such preventive goals as specific deterrence, general deterrence, and incapacitation. Punishment quickly came to be seen as a legal instrument by means of which all sorts of social benefits could be achieved—and without the harshness, arbitrariness, and discrimination that so troubled reformers like Beccaria and Bentham. Prisons soon became defined as institutions within which those goals could be pursued with reasonable efficiency and effectiveness.

This general philosophy of punishment, of course, was to be modified significantly some 100 years later when developments in the social, behavioral, and medical disciplines gave rise to the notion that offenders were really not the sorts of responsible actors about whom those advocating either retributive or utilitarian viewpoints had spoken so forcefully. Instead, beginning in the first quarter of the 19th century with regard to juvenile offenders and several decades later with regard to adult offenders, the notion that unlawful conduct was the direct product of forces over which individual offenders had little or no control—that crime was not really the product of rational actors making calculated choices for which they could and should be held responsible—began to alter the field of penology in a major fashion.

Crime prevention, to be sure, was a major goal of those associated with what came to be known as the Positive School of criminology, but gone was the fundamental thesis of the Classical School that crime prevention would become possible if we forced the "punishment to befit the crime." Instead, those who were trying to advance the cause of the so-called rehabilitative ideal contended that the proper goals of our penal system should include recognizing that offenders were not responsible for their behavior. Criminal conduct, they argued, must be seen as nothing more or less than a symptom of a condition that was to be identified, understood, and cured. Thus, distinguishing between guilt and innocence was to be the problem of the legal system. Dealing with those found guilty was to become, in effect, a problem for correctional experts who had a proper background in such fields as medicine, psychiatry, and clinical psychology.

As we have seen, one would be making a serious error by imagining that the periods of relatively recent penological history could somehow be neatly and cleanly divided into phases during which one or another perspective thoroughly dominated the field. Whether for better or worse, modern penological practice is a more or less haphazardly tossed together combination of unrelated and often quite contradictory ideas, philosophies, and practices. Some of us—private citizens as well as, for example, members of legislative bodies, the judiciary, and our "correctional establishment"—react to the tens of millions of criminal victimizations we experience each year with little more than cries for vengeance and retaliation. Others are steadfast in their advocacy for a system of justice that they see as being constructed on a purely retributive foundation. Many if not most endorse at least some of the deterrence-based ideas of the Classical School. Still others dream of the day when we will see crime as a sort of social disease that can only be addressed reasonably by one species or another of rehabilitative specialists. But even a casual observer of our system of criminal law and the penal system that it creates must recognize that what we really do is premised on the basic belief that those systems can be simultaneously retaliatory *and* retributive *and* preventive *and* rehabilitative.

Even the abbreviated review of major perspectives on punishment provided in Chapter 2 should be sufficient to show that no single system of criminal justice can hope to merge all of these very different points of view into a single unified system. (Indeed, we have seen that the problems with each viewpoint are so great that it may not be possible to create a rational system within which any one of the available perspectives can be meaningfully translated!) Yet the effort to do what theoretically and logically cannot be done persists. And then we wonder why it seems that nothing works. Having met the enemy, which is essentially little more than our own remarkable inconsistency and foolishness, we remain unable and unwilling to admit how well we know him.

Historical considerations aside, this chapter has provided us with an opportunity to review some basic information about our criminal justice system in general and our penal system in particular. This review revealed that the magnitude of the problems posed by crime today is huge. This year, for instance, nearly one-third of all households in the United States are likely to be victims of one or more criminal offenses. Even though some 50 percent of victimizations remain unreported each year, something on the order of 14 million serious felony offenses (i.e., Crime Index offenses) are likely to come to the attention of the police. Most of these—90 percent or more on average—will never work their way to a point in the criminal justice process at which any demands are placed on our correctional system. Still, we established that the load on that system is staggering: a million and a half people on some form of probation, a half a million adults serving sentences in our state and federal prisons, a quarter of a million offenders under parole supervision after receiving early releases from prison, nearly a quarter of a million persons confined in local jail facilities. Thus, as you read this chapter summary, it is almost certain that the total "correctional caseload" will be moving toward the 3 million mark.

All of this—historical considerations, legal developments, rates of crime, sentencing policies, and much more—forces our tens of thousands of correctional practitioners into an impossibly difficult position. Despite a multibillion-dollar financial resource base on which to draw, they find that those for whom they are responsible may quite reasonably be thought of as victims of our system of justice. They are asked to pursue a host of contradictory mandates within the context of a poorly integrated and insufficiently funded criminal justice system. They often think—and not without considerable justification—that they have done an adequate if not a remarkable job if they can somehow prevent offenders from becoming worse while they are under correctional supervision than they were when supervision began. A "good year" thus becomes defined not as one when indications of successful crime prevention or rehabilitative success could be identified but as one when major disturbances, riots, acts of violence, and escapes by those under supervision were kept to a minimum. Not a very positive commentary on the nature and prospects of "modern" penology, but the following chapters contain much which suggests that our problems could easily become worse before the hope of anything more positive emerges.

DISCUSSION QUESTIONS

Many early systems of law placed much importance on the obligation of an offender to his or her victim (e.g., the *wergild* payments required by early Anglo-Saxon law). Some features of this exist today in both private law (e.g., tort law) and public law (e.g., requirements for victim restitution that are incorporated into the sentences handed down by criminal court judges). Should we move even further in recognizing the plight of victims? How?

It seems almost self-evident that no system of justice can place equal importance on the goals of retaliation, retribution, crime prevention through deterrence and incapacitation, and rehabilitation. Why, then, do we continue to pretend that all of these purposes are important mandates for those working within our correctional system?

4

REHABILITATION VERSUS JUSTICE

Despite many conflicts and controversies, a way must be found to sift through the dozens of possible topics to which we might turn our attention and to identify a few major concerns that are at once substantively significant and especially revealing in what they can tell us about the present state of American penology as well as its future prospects. Criminologists differ in what they would identify as major issues, but in this and the following chapter I pursue the ones about which I have the greatest concern and personal interest. This chapter is devoted to what is quite clearly the most significant concern one can find anywhere in contemporary penology: the conflict that is raging between those who favor the traditional rehabilitative model and those who advocate one version or another of the justice model.

This selection may seem curious to those who think of penology as a field primarily committed to studying such topics as techniques of probation supervision, inmate reactions to various types of rehabilitative programs that have been implemented within institutional settings, traditional methods of parole supervision, community-based correctional initiatives, and a variety of other somewhat more tangible and matter-of-fact concerns. The criticism might even be correct if one were to define this area of criminology as one devoted exclusively to the specific strategies we devise to deal with offenders after and perhaps independent of the sentencing decisions made by our courts. However, it must be realized that such specific issues take place within a far broader legal, social, and political context. Today that broader set of contexts is in a state of rapid change. We cannot move further without considering those contexts in at least some detail.

The Rehabilitative Model versus the Justice Model

If you had to put your finger on a single feature of penological theory and practice that has had the most pervasive impact during the last decade or so, then surely your finger would point toward the life and death struggle that has been taking place between advocates of the rehabilitative model and the justice model. Sometimes with reason, usually armed with what few would define as adequate evidence to support their assertions, and almost always with a level of ideological fervor that would be the envy of a dyed-in-the-wool evangelical preacher, their heated rhetoric has filled the academic journals, dominated more than a few legislative sessions, and reshaped correctional practice in jurisdictions throughout the United States.

Fortunately, materials presented in portions of Chapters 2 and 3 introduced the basic viewpoints of those on both sides of this battle. The following paragraphs contain a quick review of ground previously covered, a modest elaboration of the earlier discussion, and a critical assessment of the advantages and limitations of the opposing viewpoints. From the beginning, however, I should note that I approach what needs to be done with grave reservations about the outcome. There are at least two reasons for my hesitancy.

First, the various versions of both the rehabilitative and the justice model are unusually slippery creatures for any who try to get a hold on them. Their advocates have made an art form out of burying all sorts of conceptual and practical problems beneath a facade of claims that they and only they have found the true road to salvation. I frankly doubt that either group has found The Final Answer. Much if not most of the rhetoric we encounter today has the outward appearance of being fresh and new, but on closer inspection one quickly learns that the bulk of it involves little more than still another effort to reinvent the wheel.

In addition, because most of what is being said in the midst of the contemporary justice model/rehabilitative model debate is limited to how we can best structure and justify the sentencing policies employed by our criminal courts, I am offended by what strikes me as the inherently conservative political bias of both opposing groups. In particular, the common assumption of each tends to be that those who are found to be guilty of unlawful conduct deserve to be defined as criminals and, therefore, that a fundamental task of criminologists specializing in penology must be to create fair and equitable methods of reacting to those who either deserve punishment (more or less the position of those associated with the justice model) or who deserve to be treated and rehabilitated (more or less the position of those favoring the rehabilitative model). By focusing attention on how to structure policies and procedures applicable to those working in the terminal phases of the criminal justice process (i.e., sentencing standards for our criminal courts and the "proper objectives" for correctional practitioners), both groups divert attention away from what I take to be more pressing concerns.

The Political Reality of Criminal Law

One of these concerns, of course, involves the manner in which we go about the business of classifying some conduct as the object of criminal law, other conduct as falling more properly into the category of various types of private law (e.g., tort law, property law, contract law, and so on), and still other conduct as being beyond the reach of both public and private law. Too often one is left with the impression that proponents of the justice and rehabilitative models see something awfully objective, crisp, and clean to this classificatory task.

They should not make so obvious a mistake. Few if any forms of conduct are obviously and objectively criminal. Even what would appear to be an especially heinous offense—criminal homicide, for instance—is not as easily defined as you might imagine. Taking the life of another—even of innocent persons—is said to be an act worthy of praise and reward in some contexts (e.g., the bombing of civilian targets in wartime situations). The same is true in more mundane and routinely encountered areas of everyday life (e.g., private citizens or law enforcement officials who kill persons who are involved in the commission of serious crimes, including a broad array of crimes for which the offenders would be entirely ineligible for sentences of death). Even when the taking of a life may not bring praise or rewards, it is often said to be justified or excusable (e.g., a person who took the life of another but who was legally insane at the time of the act, the police officer who shot an innocent person while fully believing him or her to be a dangerous criminal and who is said to have been laboring under a "reasonable mistake of fact," a person handling a pistol that he or she believed to be unloaded and who accidentally killed someone else, and so on).

Everywhere and always, in other words, what is to be and what is not to be a crime involves the fashioning of definitions and the making of hard choices. Those definitions and those choices must be made within a political context. When legislative bodies create law, they do so in a political context. When trial court judges interpret existing law, they do so in a political context. When appellate courts review either the provisions of law or the manner in which those provisions have been applied in particular cases, they do so in a political context. Inherent in those contexts are variables like competition, conflict, the values of interest groups, and power. Legal definitions, to put it a bit differently, are never matter-of-fact reflections of the "obvious criminality" of any form of conduct.

Consider what I take to be an amusing though perhaps trivial illustration of this political reality. Section 817.30 of the Florida criminal code defines "any person who willfully wears the badge, button, or other insignia of the American Legion" other than a member of the American Legion as being guilty of a misdemeanor. Is such a law reflective of the moral outrage we all experience when we see a nonmember wearing an American Legion button, or could it be that a narrowly defined interest group successfully sought to have what appears to be a fairly insignificant "right" backed by the full force and power of the state? Similarly, Section 865.02 of the Florida criminal code defines as a criminal anyone who "ships foreign-grown fruit or oranges, representing by mark or otherwise that said fruit is the product of the state." Is this, too, a reflection of the collective indignation we all experience when we learn that an orange we believe to have been grown in Florida turns out to be one grown in Israel, or could it be that Florida's criminal law seeks to protect the economic advantage of one of its major industries? Finally, since I am on the topic of Florida's citrus industry, Florida's criminal law generally deals with defining the seriousness of theft offenses by referring to the value of the stolen items (e.g., property valued at $20,000 or more is a second degree felony, property valued at more than $100 but less than $20,000 is a third degree felony, and so on (Florida Statutes Annotated, 812.014(2)(a)). Regarding citrus, however, Florida moves away from any need to assess value and simply requires its law enforcement officials to count the number of pieces of citrus that a heinous offender "knowingly obtains or uses, or endeavors to obtain or use" (Florida Statutes Annotated, 812.014(1)). "Any amount of citrus fruit consisting of 2,000 or more individual pieces of fruit" qualifies as a felony of the third degree (Florida Statutes Annotated, 814.014(2)(b)(7)).

The point, of course, is that the processes by means of which law is created must be—but often are not—defined as critically important. What is to be thought of as a crime and how things thought of as crimes are to be transformed into tight legal definitions of required or prohibited behavior are notions that involve much competition and conflict among a host of groups who seek to have their special interests, values, perceived needs, and advantages protected by the provisions of criminal law (e.g., Krisberg, 1975; Black, 1976; Hepburn, 1977; Quinney, 1979; Chambliss and Seidman, 1982; Thomas and Hepburn, 1983: 38-74). The political reality of law is often ignored in discussions of the rehabilitative and justice models.

Defects and Deficiencies in the
Criminal Justice Process

A related "blind spot" in the contemporary debate has to do with the operation of the criminal justice process. One is often left with the impression that supporters of both models seek to begin "doing justice" or "doing rehabilitation" at that point in the process where a judge in a criminal court confronts the obligation to impose a sentence. Too crudely summarized, advocates of the justice model typically contend that similar offenders convicted on similar charges must be treated fairly, equitably, and consistently. Those favoring the rehabilitative model, of course, think of the best of all possible worlds as being one within which a trial court judge would say little more to an offender than, "You are hereby committed to the care and custody of some set of correctional experts until they in their infinite wisdom decide to set you free."

While the point need not be labored over in any great detail, those who pursue either of these strategies diminish or ignore altogether the haphazard and often discriminatory influences that have shaped the criminal justice process at points prior to the time at which some judicial authority confronts an anxious offender. Think back, for instance, to our consideration of the criminal justice process in Chapter 3. Offenses are often not reported to law enforcement agencies, and those agencies seldom apprehend suspects. Prosecutors and defense counsel wheel and deal with one another both before and after the high drama of a courtroom setting materializes.

In the midst of it all, a majority of all offenders either escape an encounter with the criminal justice process altogether or, having encountered it, find a way to escape any true threat to life or liberty by dropping through one of its dozens of cracks. Even those whose initial luck is less than good are commonly able to strike one type of bargain or another if, for example, they cooperate by entering a plea of guilty rather than exercising their constitutional right to a full-scale trial (e.g., Alschuler, 1978; Bureau of Justice Statistics, 1984d). For a host of reasons—to speed up the criminal justice process, to lighten the load on bulging criminal court dockets, to compensate for known weaknesses in their cases, to modify provisions of criminal law to suit personal preferences, and many more—deals are made and bargains struck. It happens thousands of times each day and with what amounts to the full knowledge and prior approval of our appellate courts (e.g., *North Carolina v. Pearce*, 395 U.S. 711, 1969; *Brady v.*

United States, 397 U.S. 742, 1970; *Bordenkircher v. Hayes*, 434 U.S. 357, 1978). True, in *Bordenkircher* and elsewhere the U.S. Supreme Court has recognized that "there is no doubt that the breadth of discretion that our country's legal system vests in prosecuting attorneys carries with it the potential for both individual and institutional abuse." If nothing else, however, the court remains mindful of the practical advantages of our system of bargained justice. In *Santobello v. New York* (404 U.S. 257, 1971), for example, Chief Justice Burger concluded:

> The disposition of criminal charges by agreement between the prosecutor and the accused, sometimes loosely called plea bargaining, is an essential component of the administration of justice. Properly administered, it is to be encouraged. If every criminal charge were subject to a full scale trial, the States and the Federal government would need to multiply by many times the number of judges and court facilities.

The result is something of a shell game. You accept my bargain and I'll transform your burglary into a less serious charge of breaking and entering. You accept my bargain and I'll pretend that your aggravated rape was only an aggravated assault. You accept my bargain and I'll conclude that the gun in your possession at the time of your offense never existed. You accept my bargain and I'll recommend a term on probation rather than a prison sentence. Often, however, all of the wheeling and dealing disappears when those seeking a reform of sentencing policies and objectives go to work. The silliness of it all has not escaped notice. Consider, for instance, the following comments from an essay by Alschuler (1978: 69-70):

> The *laissez-faire* attitude of sentencing reformers toward this concentration of governmental power in prosecutors' offices is probably not the product of blindness or indifference. It is probably best explained by a pervasive sense that, for one reason or another, the institution of plea bargaining is impregnable. The reformers may have accepted the claim that trial courts would be swamped if the power to bargain for guilty pleas were substantially restricted, or they may have nodded at assurances that efforts to restrict the bargaining process would merely drive it underground. Moreover, the reformers probably have little desire to engage in what they see as a fruitless political battle ... [but] I am not at all persuaded that our society is too impoverished to give its criminal defendants their day in court. Most nations of the world, including many far poorer than ours, do manage to resolve their criminal cases without bargaining. ... I believe that the political battle could be won if

those who recognize the injustice of our current regime of prosecutorial power would simply fight the fight.

In short, today we routinely encounter heated debates between supporters of the rehabilitative and justice models. Those in both groups have sincere concerns, concerns that deserve careful and thorough attention. In their zeal to lobby effectively for their respective positions, however, they frequently fall into the trap of being unable to see the forest for the trees. Any temptation to be equally myopic and to conclude that agreeing on sentencing policies and their goals is either the first or the most important step we must take in creating a more enlightened penal system must be studiously avoided.

THE REHABILITATIVE IDEAL

Depending in part on which of several points of view one might wish to accept, the argument can be made that enthusiasm for rehabilitation as a major objective of penal sanctions dates back to the time of Plato or before. One could also select any number of somewhat more recent starting points. The conversion of the Bridewell Place into an at least partly reform-oriented prison in 1555 might be one possibility. The popularization of the idea toward the end of the 18th century that prisons could be used to confine convicted offenders rather than largely as places where they could be confined until they could be put on trial or until some other sentence (e.g., branding, banishment, and execution) could be carried out would be another alternative. Such choices, however, would force us to equate the rehabilitative model with any and all efforts to respond to offenders with the hope of changing them in any way by any means with an application of the rehabilitative model.

So global a definition of the rehabilitative model strikes me as having few if any merits. Given the core assertions of the rehabilitative model, it is virtually impossible to imagine it having any true role to play in penological history until one essential development materialized: Notions of individual responsibility for criminal conduct— notions that are of central importance to those who advance either retributive or utilitarian perspectives on punishment—had to be challenged by those who hypothesized that offenders cannot and should not be held personally responsible for their actions because they have little if any personal control over their behavior.

As we have seen, various theories more or less compatible with this disavowal of individual responsibility became relatively common during the initial decades of the 19th century. Some of these strike most criminologists of today as being almost bizarre (e.g., the "lumps and bumps" theories of the phrenologists). Others contain ideas remarkably similar to many contemporary perspectives (e.g., the work of Quetelet and other members of the Statistical or Ecological School of criminology). However, with the possible exception of the House of Refuge movement that was aimed at treatment of juvenile offenders, a movement that dates back to roughly 1825, it seems most accurate to conclude that the practical beginnings of the rehabilitative model were linked to developments that unfolded in the clinical and behavioral sciences during the last quarter of the 19th century—most particularly developments in the field of criminology (with the establishment of the Positive School) and medicine (with the growing recognition accorded to psychiatry).

The basic thesis of those who advocate the rehabilitative model is already familiar. First, they define as inappropriate and misleading any and all efforts to use such concepts as "justice" and "just punishment." Whether used by retributivists or utilitarians, such terms presuppose a rational actor having made a conscious choice to engage in unlawful conduct, a choice for which punishment should be imposed if justice is to be done. Some years ago, for example, Karl Menninger (1968: 17) made this quite explicit:

> The very word *justice* irritates scientists. No surgeon expects to be asked if an operation for cancer is just or not. No doctor will be reproached on the grounds that the dose of penicillin he has prescribed is less or more than *justice* would stipulate.

> Behavioral scientists regard it as equally absurd to invoke the question of justice in deciding what to do with a woman who cannot resist her propensity to shoplift, or with a man who cannot repress an impulse to assault somebody. This sort of behavior has to be controlled; it has to be discouraged; it has to be *stopped*. This (to the scientist) is a matter of public safety and amicable coexistence, not of justice [emphasis in original].

Second, as is made obvious by Menninger's statement, the proper objective of sentencing is not to impose punishment based on notions of either just desert or deterrence. The initial objective is to understand that crime is a symptom of the underlying disorder which produced it. We do not punish cancer patients harshly because of the seriousness of their disease or the difficulty of preventing its recurrence in the future. Neither do we necessarily avoid the infliction of pain on those with nothing more serious than cavities in their teeth because of some idea that nonserious symptoms require nonserious responses. Instead, we collect and analyze data regarding a patient's condition, we make a diagnosis, we formulate a treatment plan, and we then get on with the business of curing.

The third feature of the rehabilitative model is largely predetermined by the first two. If justice is an irrelevant term, and if intervention aimed at diagnosing and then treating offenders is to be the true objective of a new generation of correctional practitioners, then those lacking the necessary clinical expertise must take the first step. They must create the proper therapeutic context within which the medical miracles are later to reveal themselves. Other than the obvious features of this first step (e.g., providing needed physical facilities, personnel, and so on), it requires what amounts to one major leap of faith. It requires that our system of criminal law remove any and all linkages between the nature of crimes committed and the nature of sentences imposed.

As the broad appeal of the rehabilitative model gained strength during the first half of the 20th century, efforts to meet this requirement began to materialize in several significant forms. They can be divided into two broad categories. One involved sentencing standards and policies as they revealed themselves in the context of criminal courts. One jurisdiction after another moved away from imposing a fixed or determinate sentence on convicted offenders (i.e., a requirement that an offender be confined for a term highly correlated with the legal seriousness of his or her offense). Instead, those whose rehabilitation was not deemed to require confinement increasingly found themselves being placed on probation, a judicial disposition that permitted them to escape harsher treatment as long as they abided by the various conditions imposed by such a disposition (e.g., Diana, 1960; Carter and Wilkins, 1970; Cavender, 1982). Others encountered one of several types of sentencing policies aimed in whole or in part at facilitating rehabilitative efforts.

At least three general forms of such sentencing policies became popular: *indeterminate sentences, maximum only sentences,* and *minimum-maximum sentences.* Those receiving an indeterminate sentence remained under correctional supervision until correctional "experts" determined that they had been rehabilitated. For advocates of the rehabilitative model, this continues to be seen as the only really meaningful sentencing scheme. Those sentenced under a maximum only standard would enter the correctional system knowing that they could serve no more than a fixed amount of time but also that they could be released at any point prior to the expiration date of their sentence if correctional officials determined that early release decisions were in order. Finally, those sentenced under a minimum-maximum scheme would be in substantially the same position as those sentenced under the maximum only approach, with the exception that correctional officials could not release them until they had served some minimum portion of their sentence. Differences between the three sentencing models, of course, could be either considerable or minimal. For example, a fully indeterminate sentence, a maximum only sentence set at 50 years, and a minimum-maximum sentence set at no less than one nor more than 50 years in prison all mean substantially the same thing in many important regards.

The other category—parole—involves decisions by nonjudicial authorities, but it is implicit in the logic of what has just been reviewed. Just as advocates of the rehabilitative model contend that sentencing decisions regarding who should and should not be confined should flow primarily from treatment considerations rather than offense seriousness, they also argue that prison release decisions must come from expert assessments of rehabilitative progress rather than from rigid legal standards. Offenders, they suggest, should be confined only until their progress in treatment programs demonstrates their readiness for release. Thus, a mechanism to free rehabilitated offenders at virtually any point during their period of correctional involvement is said to be essential. Parole provides such a release mechanism. Parole involves an administrative determination, presumably by properly qualified correctional experts, that a particular offender has made such rehabilitative progress that he or she no longer presents a serious risk to the community. Early release on parole, however, is a conditional release. Parolees are required to remain under the supervision of parole officers and to meet any obligations their parole agreements impose on them. Failure to meet such obligations can result in parole revocation and a return to prison.

Evaluating the Rehabilitative Ideal

Especially during the period of roughly 1880 through 1960, support for the rehabilitative model was substantial among large numbers of academics, politicians, upper-level correctional administrators, and a significant fraction of the general public. Its impact on the routine operation of our penal system, however, was much less evident. Gradually, cracks in the base of support for the rehabilitative model began to form, cracks that continue to broaden as this is being written. At least five fundamental criticisms warrant mention here.

First, the rehabilitative model is defective on both a conceptual and a practical level. Its advocates urge us to think of offenders as people who are suffering from a disease that can be identified, diagnosed, and successfully treated. One might quickly stipulate that this could be true with regard to some small fraction of all offenders. However, in the vast majority of cases there is no indication of any physical or mental disease. Moreover, there is little or no indication that those in the clinical or behavioral sciences have reached a point in the development of their respective specialties that they have the "people-processing technology" that is required to transform their human subjects from some rough "raw material" state into some acceptable "final product." Indeed, they have not yet reached a point at which they can specify with any real clarity what they mean by a "rehabilitated offender." Consequently, the rehabilitative concept urges us to think of offenders as being persons who suffer from some disease, defect, or disorder in the absence of acceptable scientific evidence that their concept is valid for more than a small proportion of offenders. They then promise to "cure" offenders, even though virtually all available evidence suggests that viable strategies for coerced treatment—inmates are hardly to be thought of as voluntary patients—do not exist (e.g., Morris, 1974; Lipton et al., 1975; Thomas and Petersen, 1977).

Second, to the extent that rehabilitative efforts can be viewed as appropriate in some contexts—most of which have far more to do with vocational and educational training than with some type of clinical intervention—it is very unlikely that successes can be achieved when rehabilitative involvements are forced rather than voluntary (e.g., Morris, 1974). This widely recognized reality seems to have escaped many advocates of the rehabilitative model, but it remains true nonetheless. The simple fact seems to be that meaningful changes in attitudes, behavior, and world views are most likely to materialize when those to be changed are actively and positively involved in the change process. Most applications of the rehabilitative model make such voluntary participation all but impossible. When, for example, the possibility for early release from confinement on parole is tied to participation in various types of rehabilitative programs, how can it be said that participation is voluntary? Clearly it is not, and it probably cannot be made to become either voluntary or effective within the context of the present system.

Third, much of what we see today is based on the belief that correctional practitioners are able to measure responsiveness to rehabilitative initiatives and to use appropriate measures to set release dates. Virtually all available evidence, however, questions their ability to predict who will or will not become reinvolved in criminal behavior after release from correctional supervision. Any efforts to do so are, among other things, undermined by what are often referred to as *false positive* and *false negative* predictions of future dangerousness (Wilkins, 1969; von Hirsch, 1976; Morris and Miller, 1985). False positive predictions occur when those who are predicted to be poor risks do not behave in accordance with such predictions. False negative predictions occur when those who are said to be a good risks prove to be dangerous. The problem is that we have never been very successful in predicting postrelease behavior. The most common adjustment we have made has involved overpredicting future dangerousness. At the logical extreme, for instance, if we predicted that everyone who was released from correctional supervision would become reinvolved in crime, we would never see a single case of any offender becoming reinvolved in crime that we did not predict would do so. This "safe and accurate" approach, however, would necessarily create a huge number of false positive predictions. In other words, we might well confine large numbers of people for considerable periods of time on the basis of our prediction that releasing them would be dangerous when in fact they would have posed no risk of dangerousness had they been released much earlier.

Fourth, given the present debate between those favoring the rehabilitative or the justice model, one might well assume that those in the former group are trying to avoid some abolition of the rehabilitative programs they have fought so long and hard to establish. Tears, however, do not come to the eyes of those who know anything about the everyday operation of our penal system. A plain and simple fact of life that is known to all but the most naive is that the rehabilitative model has seldom if ever been implemented in a meaningful fashion. True, many pages ago I noted that it is relatively easy to call the penal system a correctional system, to call prison guards correctional officers, and to refer to everything from solitary confinement to wacking away at the weeds on a prison farm as parts of a rehabilitative program. Nevertheless, meaningful translations of the rehabilitative theory into actual practice are about as easy to find today as live dinosaurs. Regardless of whether we deal with programs of 100 years ago or those of today, the prime objective is invariably one of control and never one of change. Prisons provide the most obvious illustration of this reality. The goal is and has long been one of maintaining custodial control (e.g., preventing violence, preventing major disturbances such as riots, preventing escapes, and so on).

Even the most committed and traditional supporters of the rehabilitative ideal are fully aware of the fact that their theory remains untranslated into actual practice. Almost but not quite amusingly, they counter the justice model advocates with two awfully transparent contentions—neither of which, conveniently enough, is subject to proof or disproof. One such contention seeks to wrap the rehabilitative model in the holy cloth of humanitarianism (e.g., Cressey, 1982). Who, after all, would loudly proclaim his or her flat rejection of and opposition to humanitarian principles? True, they admit, the rehabilitative model may be defective and, in any event, may have seldom if ever been adopted as a real guide for penal practice. Still, they ask, is not the true value of the model to be found in its having promoted a more humane system? This viewpoint suffers from two fatal problems: (1) A slow drift toward more humane responses to offenders began long before rather than as a consequence of the development of the rehabilitative model, and (2) contrary to assertions made by people like Cressey, no responsible group in the nation is presently advocating a policy of terror and brutality.

The other contention is that we should not move away from rehabilitative strategies until they have been given a full and fair opportunity to work. More than a hundred years of tinkering and billions of dollars in expenditures are presumably not sufficient to reveal anything. The circular illogic of this argument is obvious. How would we know that the rehabilitative model had been given a fair chance? When it had not yet produced the desired results, of course. Those who accept such crisp and clean logic tend also to be favorably inclined when they are invited to purchase the Brooklyn Bridge at a discount price.

Finally, there is something of a "breach of promise" problem that one encounters in examining the rehabilitative model. The promise is and has long been that the investment of broad and unreviewable discretionary powers in correctional experts would pave the road to rehabilitative success. The public, members of legislative bodies, and trial court judges, we are told, appreciate that they have neither the training nor the special expertise of physicians. Therefore, such nonexperts do not tell physicians how to go about the business of practicing medicine. The same strategy, it is argued, should extend to correctional practice. Perhaps it is the role of law to define who is eligible for correctional treatment, but all that follows such a definition is said to be the province of experts. If such policies have the result of two apparently similar offenders serving vastly different sentences, if they sometimes have the consequence of appearing to treat very serious offenders quite leniently, if they equally often result in those who appear to have committed nonserious offenses remaining under correctional supervision for very long periods of time, or if a host of other things that seem contrary to simple notions of justice materialize, then nonexperts are to satisfy themselves that whatever is happening is doing so in the service of a worthy quasi-medical objective.

The simple and obvious reality is that the promise has never been kept. Correctional practitioners have enjoyed vast amounts of discretionary power, power that has been nearly immune from any sort of review when offenders have claimed that the system has dealt with them unreasonably or unfairly. But study after study has shown that the rhetoric of rehabilitation has promised much while delivering pitifully little (e.g., Bailey, 1966; Morris, 1974; Lerman, 1975; Lipton et al., 1975; Riedel and Thornberry, 1978).

THE JUSTICE MODEL

Criticisms of the rehabilitative model notwithstanding, advocating it came close to being a nearly automatic response for several generations of criminologists. Understanding why is not especially difficult. To begin with, criminologists are behavioral scientists. They firmly believe that all human behavior is caused. The rehabilitative model also conceptualizes human behavior as being caused (as opposed, for example to it representing a course of action that is chosen by individuals endowed with a "free will"). Second, like most other species of academics, criminologists tend to be liberal in terms of their philosophical and political preferences. To the extent that favoring the punishment of offenders for any reason is often thought to reflect a philosophically or politically conservative position, the fact that the rehabilitative model flatly rejects punishment as a proper goal of punishment elevates its appeal. Third, criminologists are certainly not immune from social and political pressures which say, in effect, that all scientific disciplines are valuable if and only if they contribute to the resolution of those social problems which fall within the scope of their respective areas of expertise. Rushing to gain the prestige accorded those in other disciplines (e.g., physics, chemistry, biology, and so on), the "expert status" assigned to at least some types of criminologists by the rehabilitative model was hardly unwelcome. Virtually everyone, after all, enjoys thinking that they are important, that they have some special expertise to offer, and that they can use their expertise to improve the human condition. (In addition, those with even the most superficial contacts with the academic world are well aware of the fact that academic egos are seldom small!)

Despite these and other bonds between many criminologists and the rehabilitative model, over the past decade or so more and more of them—along with legislative bodies, members of the judiciary, correctional practitioners, and the public at large—have found themselves being attracted to one or more versions of what is most commonly referred to today as the justice model (e.g., American Friends Service Committee, 1971; Morris, 1974; Fogel, 1975; van den Haag, 1975; von Hirsch, 1976; Twentieth Century Fund, 1976; Fogel and Hudson, 1981; Gross and von Hirsch, 1981). On a very general level, the justice model can be thought of as a critical reaction both to perceived defects in the rehabilitative model and to the way in which the model has been translated into correctional practice. However, on closer inspection one quickly finds that there are a number of rather different justice models to which a single name has been attached.

One of these versions of the justice model deserves and will receive little attention here. Its advocates include a diverse array of conservative politicians who long ago learned that few things play quite as well to the folks back home as "get tough on crime" planks in political platforms, significant numbers of private citizens who have accepted the misguided belief that harsh sentences and crime prevention are virtually one and the same thing, and more than a few academics—Ernest van den Haag being perhaps the most widely recognized member of this group—who have learned that the financial rewards of crime and punishment can be substantial if you say popular things about them. With or without some superficial use of fancy philosophical or criminological jargon, their "vengeance can be fun and profitable" perspective on penology is worth a little more than a bit of space on a sticker for the bumper of a dusty pick-up truck. There are, however, more thoughtful points of view that do deserve our attention and careful consideration.

The Problems and Consequences of Unbridled Discretion

Although a thorough examination of the more thoughtful statements of the justice model would reveal significant differences, two common denominators seem quite clear. One of these is a pervasive concern with the consequences of how discretionary powers are used within our criminal justice system, especially discretionary powers that are vested in members of the judiciary. If we consider historical data on sentencing, comparisons of sentencing policies across jurisdictions (i.e., the federal criminal courts compared with overall state criminal court information or interstate comparisons), or data on sentencing within the various courts of a single jurisdiction (e.g., cross-country or cross-judicial circuit comparisons with a particular state), we consistently find one reality that should concern us all (e.g., Pope, 1975; Sutton, 1978; Bureau of Justice Statistics, 1984g; Brown et al., 1984: 504-505; Zatz, 1984, 1985). There are wild fluctuations in the likelihood and harshness of the sentences our criminal courts impose.

Some of these disparities, of course, stem from the seriousness of the offenses under consideration and the prior criminal records of those who are being sentenced. An unknown fraction of them may reflect efforts to tailor sentences to the perceived rehabilitative needs of defendants. Beyond these sorts of influences, however, many of the sentencing variations have been related to such factors as the social and demographic characteristics of defendants (e.g., age, sex, race, employment status, income, rural versus urban place of residence, marital status, and so on). It is difficult if not impossible to view variations in sentences that flow from such influences as reflecting nothing more than sound efforts to tailor sentencing decisions to the special rehabilitative needs of individual offenders. Furthermore, additional influences include type of counsel (appointed versus private defense attorneys), the social and demographic characteristics of trial court judges, the number of criminal cases on trial court dockets, and public reactions to particular offenses or offenders.

Sentencing disparities associated with these types of variables clearly have nothing whatsoever to do with translating rehabilitative theory into sound sentencing practice. In the hundreds of sentencing studies that have been reported over the past half century or so, I am not aware of a single research report in which more than a modest percentage of variations in sentencing has been explained, even when researchers incorporated large numbers of potential influences into their analyses. The clear implication seems to be that much of what influences sentencing decisions by trial court judges is so haphazard, random, and capricious that researchers who are attempting to identify a regular and routine pattern are looking for something that often does not exist. (Lawyers who specialize in criminal cases, of course, have long known that the fate of their clients often depends on little more or less than the mood of a given judge on a given day and such legally irrelevant factors as a trial court judge's ever-changing attitudes toward particular offenses, particular prosecutors, and particular defense counsel.)

Advocates of the justice model are uniform in their criticism of each and every one of these influences on sentencing decisions. Some of the influences reveal unconstitutional patterns of discrimination. Others suggest that sentencing decisions have been as much a chance-based lottery as an even-handed distribution of justice. Others make it clear that our trial courts will do what needs to be done to move cases through our overcrowded system with little regard for how the movement of those cases is accomplished. Still others indicate some degree of effort to relate sentencing decisions to the likelihood of rehabilitation in the almost total absence of sound empirical evidence linking variations in sentencing to variations in rehabilitative success. Where, they ask, is the justice in such a haphazard and often discriminatory system? Where is the mechanism that guarantees that more or less similar offenders will be treated in a more or less similar fashion as they move through the criminal justice system?

Suffice it to say that they find no such mechanism, that they see little in our legal system that translates justice into the fair, equitable, or predictable treatment of defendants. Many of them go on to demand an end to unbridled discretion and the creation of new sentencing policies that are capable of controlling it. (At this point it is important to recall the earlier criticism regarding the inappropriateness of concentrating too much attention on sentencing to the exclusion of granting sufficient importance to the presentencing phases of the criminal justice process.) Although there are almost as many specific strategies for achieving this objective as there are advocates of the justice model, at least two general approaches warrant mention here: determinate or presumptive sentencing models and sentencing guidelines models. Understand, however, that the criminal codes of the individual states and of the federal government routinely create huge numbers of complex qualifications and exceptions to what is described below.

The Presumptive Sentence Strategy

Determinate or *presumptive sentencing models* can be described fairly concisely. The basic thesis is that the legislative rather than the judicial branch of government has the responsibility for creating criminal law and providing forms of punishment for those who violate the provisions of criminal law. If the legislative branch delegates its constitutional powers to the judicial branch by creating what were described previously as indeterminate, maximum only, or minimum-maximum sentencing provisions, then the legislative branch has opened the door through which wide sentencing disparities are likely to come. Advocates of presumptive sentencing argue that a simple way of resolving the problem requires nothing more than convincing legislators to do what they were supposed to be doing all along (i.e., to attach a fixed punishment to each offense or category of offenses). Trial court judges would then be responsible for conducting the business of their courts and, when a defendant was found guilty, imposing whatever sentence was required by law.

While advocates of the justice model have reshaped the sentencing landscapes in a host of criminal codes throughout the United States, no jurisdiction has adopted policies that totally remove all sentencing discretion from trial court judges. Presumptive sentencing models, however, are attracting a good deal of attention. California provides perhaps the best known illustration. Explicitly declaring, for example, that "the purpose of imprisonment for crime is punishment" and that "this purpose is best served by terms proportionate to the seriousness of the offense with provisions for uniformity in the sentences of offenders committing the same offense under similar circumstances" (California Penal Code, Section 1170), California moved into the presumptive sentencing camp.

In its revised criminal code, California criminal law provides for prison terms of three, five, or seven years for some offenses. California law holds that "When a judgment of imprisonment is to be imposed and the statute specifies three possible terms, the court shall order the imposition of the middle term, unless there are circumstances in aggravation or mitigation of the crime" (California Penal Code, Section 1170(b)). Thus, a sentence of five years would be the presumptive sentence. However, either the prosecutor or the defense counsel would have an opportunity to introduce relevant aggravating or mitigating evidence. Sufficient aggravating factors could lead to a sentence of seven years; sufficient mitigating factors could lead to a sentence of three years. California goes even further in its quest for greater uniformity in sentencing by requiring that its Board of Prison Terms review the cases of all persons who are imprisoned within one year of their being confined. The object of the review is to determine whether each sentence is reasonably consistent "in comparison with the sentences imposed in similar cases" (California Penal Code, Section 1170(f) (1)). The Board of Prison Terms can require a resentencing hearing if unreasonable disparities are detected.

Limiting Discretion through Sentencing Guidelines

An increasingly popular alternative to limiting judicial discretion in sentencing is provided by *sentencing guidelines models* of the type now being used in Minnesota, Florida, and many other jurisdictions. The general goal of those adopting the sentencing guidelines approach is substantially the same as those favoring presumptive sentences. In Florida, for example, the purpose of sentencing is "to establish a uniform set of standards to guide the sentencing judge in the sentence decision-making process," and the sentencing guidelines "are intended to eliminate unwarranted variation in the sentencing process by reducing the subjectivity in interpreting specific offense- and offender-related criteria and in defining their relative importance in sentencing decision" (Rule 3.701(b), Florida Rules of Criminal Procedure). In addition, Florida, not unlike dozens of states in which presumptive sentencing or sentencing guidelines models have been put forward, flatly rejects the hypothesis that the primary purpose of sentencing is rehabilitative. Instead, "the primary purpose of sentencing is to punish the offender. Rehabilitation and other traditional considerations continue to be desired goals of the criminal justice system but most assume a subordinate role" (Rule 3.701(b) (2), Florida Rules of Criminal Procedure).

The mechanical aspects of sentencing guidelines are easy enough to describe. Those used by Florida provide as good an example as those of any other state. First, a guidelines scoresheet is prepared by the prosecutor. These scoresheets are forms that have been created for each of the nine categories into which all criminal offenses have been subdivided (e.g., Category 1 includes murder and manslaughter, Category 2 includes sexual offenses, Category 6 includes thefts, forgery, and fraud, and Category 9 includes all felony offenses not found in the first eight categories). Several fairly matter-of-fact questions are posed to the prosecutor as he or she completes the form. What is the most serious offense of which this person has been convicted? Was he or she also convicted on some other charge (e.g., both murder and armed robbery)? What is the nature of the offender's prior criminal record (evidence regarding the offender's juvenile record is relevant if juvenile offenses came within the past three years)? Was the offender under some type of supervision at the time of the most recent offense (e.g., probation or parole)? If the offense is a crime against a person, what was the nature of the harm done to the victim(s)?

The answer to each of these types of questions is worth a certain number of points. Thus, when the prosecutor has completed the sentencing guidelines form, he or she adds up all of the relevant point information. A table is provided for each of the nine offense categories. It translates point totals into a "sentencing guidelines range." For example, a person convicted of burglary whose guidelines scoresheet total was between 121 and 143 points would have what amounts to a presumptive sentence of six years in prison. The trial court judge, however, could impose a sentence of anything between five and one-half years and seven years (the sentencing guidelines range). Florida did not wish to eliminate judicial discretion: "The sentencing guidelines are designed to aid the judge in the sentencing decision and are not intended to usurp judicial discretion" (Rule 3.701(b) (6), Florida Rules of Criminal Procedure). Thus, trial court judges in Florida may ignore the guideline sentence and impose whatever more lenient or harsher punishment may be permitted by law if they so desire. When they do so, however, they must provide "clear and convincing reasons to warrant aggravating or mitigating the [guideline] sentence" (Rule 3.701(d) (11), Florida Rules of Criminal Procedure). Furthermore, any departure from guideline sentences may be reviewed by an appellate court on the motion of either the prosecutor or the defense counsel. Consequently, roughly 80 percent of the sentences handed down in Florida's criminal courts since the sentencing guidelines model was adopted in 1983 have been consistent with the guidelines recommendations. (I should hasten to add that Florida's appellate courts have been willing to accept almost any trial court rationale for ignoring guidelines recommendations as satisfying the "clear and convincing reasons" standard.)

The most important point for this discussion, of course, is not the particular strategy that individual jurisdictions may adopt to limit judicial discretion, but whether there is a trend toward limiting it in some fashion. Advocates of the rehabilitative model strongly oppose creating any such limits. (Actually, they oppose any judicial discretion and favor instead of fully indeterminate sentences, but this reality is often lost in the midst of the battles we are witnessing today.) Proponents of the justice model see something akin to presumptive sentencing or guidelines sentencing models as the only practical way of bringing fairness, equity, and predictability of sentencing back into the criminal justice process. The harshness of the sentences that often flow from revised sentencing models is a growing source of concern among many who favor the justice model approach, but it seems even more apparent that those who support the traditional rehabilitative model are losing almost every battle they confront.

Linking Prison Release Dates to
Rehabilitative Progress

As indicated earlier, the multiple versions of the justice model seem to have two common denominators. Unbridled judicial discretion is the one that has attracted the greater amount of attention, but the justice model criticism of efforts to relate length of time under correctional supervision to rehabilitative progress is no less important.

The basic question is quite simple: Once a trial court judge has imposed a sentence on a convicted offender, under what if any circumstances should that sentence be subject to modification by a nonjudicial authority? At least in terms of the past practices of our penal system, we have answered this question affirmatively and have relied on two different methods of sentence modification. One of these is associated with what is typically referred to a *good time* or *gain time* credit. Computations of such "time off for good behavior" provisions vary from one jurisidiction to the next. A Florida inmate, for instance, can "earn" a sentence reduction of from 5 to 15 days per month served during which he or she "has committed no infraction of the rules or regulations of the division [of corrections], or the laws of the state, and...has performed in a faithful, diligent, industrious, orderly, and peaceful manner, the work, duties, and tasks" assigned to him or her (Florida Statutes Annotated, Section 944.27 (1)).

This method of sentence modification has not been the object of much dispute. Although legal provisions of the type just quoted may make it seem that good time or gain time is a reward that must be earned, the fact of the matter is that most prison officials and prison inmates see time off for good behavior as a right that should not be tampered with unless there is clear evidence of serious misconduct. The real dispute has been over the various means that jurisdictions have created to grant inmates early release on parole. Parole, of course, has long been seen as a vital tool by advocates of the rehabilitative model. They argue that broadly discretionary parole release provisions permit them to release offenders from institutions at the precise point at which sufficient rehabilitative progress has been made. It is entirely unreasonable, they contend, to retain a person in prison when he or she has been responsive to rehabilitative efforts when we justify their imprisonment as a means of pursuing rehabilitative goals.

This position infuriates those favoring the justice model (e.g., Morris, 1974; Cavender, 1982). First of all, they point to a considerable literature that reveals that rehabilitative efforts in general, and parole in particular, have proven to be unsuccessful (e.g., Kassenbaum et al., 1971). Second, they argue that the processes by which eligibility for parole are determined by members of parole boards are at least as haphazard and discriminatory as the worst manifestations of unbridled judicial discretion (e.g., Blalock, 1981; Stanley, 1981). Despite the obvious gravity and hypothetical complexity of the decision that board members must make, it is not at all uncommon for them to allocate five to ten minutes per case in order to process the dozens of cases that may be on their schedule for a single day (Stanley, 1981: 235). Third, a nearly universal criticism of all who have had any contact with parole proceedings is that board members quite openly and routinely put themselves in the position of prosecutors and trial court judges. I have interviewed dozens of inmates, for instance, during whose parole hearings questions were asked about their "real offenses" as opposed to the offenses for which they were actually convicted. If parole board members concluded that the prosecutor had filed too lenient or too harsh a charge, or that the trial court judge had imposed too lenient or too harsh a sentence, they felt perfectly free to adjust the sentence to suit their personal definitions of justice by either granting or refusing an early release via parole. Generally speaking, therefore, those favoring the justice model recommend that traditional methods of granting parole be abolished or, if retained, subjected to very careful constraints.

Evaluating the Justice Model Alternative

Trying to evaluate the justice model is a difficult task. Part of the reason for the difficulty, of course, is that "doing justice" has come to mean so many different things to so many diferent people. In addition, much of what has been said by various advocates of one type of justice model has been said as much as a hostile critique of the abuses and failures of the rehabilitative model as in support of a clearly conceptualized alternative to it. Nevertheless, some general evaluative comments seem to be in order.

First, the roots of the justice model grew from the work of scholars who had become convinced that decades of efforts to work with the rehabilitative model had produced no positive benefits but much abusive exercise of the broad discretionary powers that had been granted to those responsible for administering the components of our criminal justice system. These liberal (e.g., Morris, 1974) and sometimes radical (e.g., American Friends Service Committee, 1971) critics saw the need for sweeping changes in how we make and use criminal law, how we process offenders through the criminal justice system, and what we seek to gain by the often harsh types of sentences we impose on those convicted of unlawful conduct. They imagined a fundamentally different system within which political repression, racism, and unfairness would be replaced reason and justice. Moreover, they saw a need for such changes within both the larger society and all components of the criminal justice system.

Somewhere along the way, however, the reform agenda became far more simplistic and more narrowly focused (e.g., Greenberg and Humphries, 1980). The call for major efforts to reform fundamental features of the structure of society—including significant changes in the distribution of economic and political power—seems never to have been heard. Recommendations for equally major adjustments in how we use and what we expect from our body of criminal law found much scholarly but very little political support. Instead, time after time the public and political agenda came to focus primarily on changing narrow features of the sentencing policies on which we had relied previously and secondarily on modest adjustments in the powers allocated to such groups as those responsible for parole systems. The original spirit—and perhaps the true potential for significant reform—quickly began to wither away.

In short, much of what we are witnessing today has little to do either with justice or the more thoughtful versions of the justice model. It has to do instead with various conservative groups using the liberal rhetoric of the justice model as they go about the business of taking discretionary powers away from the judiciary—a group they have always suspected of being "soft on crime"—and correctional practitioners—a group they have often described (quite incorrectly) as being dominated by "bleeding heart liberals." The consequence has often been that more offenders find themselves confronting longer prison terms. Even where substantial changes have been accomplished in, for example, sentencing policies, what we are most commonly seeing today is that the potential and the reality of an abusive use of power has moved from the courtroom to the legislative chamber. It is hard to imagine that the victims of such abuse have a preference for either type of injustice.

This, of course, is the opposite of what justice model advocates recommend. They consistently urged policies that would call for the greatest possible reliance on alternatives to prison sentences and for much shorter terms of confinement for those who were incarcerated. When other results are produced—when, for example, new sentencing policies recommend or require prison terms for a smaller number of offenders—the reason almost invariably has more to do with financial considerations than with lofty principles of justice.

Second, there is more to the present situation than radical and liberal reformers experiencing a bit of cooptation at the hands of their conservative opponents. More than a few justice model proponents simply became deafened by the sound of their own rhetoric. It is one thing to speak in terms of fairness, equity, and justice; it is an altogether different thing to translate such concepts into the more practical terms of everyday life. Sentencing standards are but the most obvious example of this problem. To create a new sentencing system that is fair, equitable, and just presupposes that there are tangible, specific flaws in the existing system and that there are equally specific adjustments that should be made to remedy these flaws.

Justice model proponents have been quite effective in identifying specific flaws and, at least in some ways, in coming forward with procedures that might remedy them (e.g., presumptive and sentencing guidelines models). However, they have fallen short in the area of precise and thoroughly justified recommendations for sentencing policies. Like the retributivists with whom some of them identify, they are necessarily vague and ambiguous regarding what a given offense or offender deserves. Too often, as in California and Florida, their quest for fairness and equity has led them to look to little more than past sentencing practices. If, for instance, historical sentencing data reveal an average sentence of x years in prison for offense y, then some contend that it is only reasonable to use this average sentence as the presumptive or guideline sentence. The absurdity of this approach should be painfully obvious. If one bases a hostile critique of the existing system on the bias and discrimination of past practice, how can one reasonbly argue that the average value of that past practice is now to be seen as just?

SUMMARY

This chapter has been devoted to an examination and assessment of the heated battle that is now raging between two groups whose perspective on correctional philosophy and practice is vastly different. Those favoring the traditional rehabilitative model continue to argue that crime is best conceptualized as a symptom of an individual offender's defect, disease, or disorder. Punishment, they argue, is appropriate only when we are convinced that those receiving it are fully responsible for their harmful conduct. In the absence of clear and convincing evidence of individual responsibility, our obligation is to intervene purely to provide the types of rehabilitative treatment that will at once cure the underlying cause of the offensive conduct and prevent its recurrence in the future. In contrast, those advocating the justice model have come forward with persuasive evidence that the rehabilitative model is fundamentally defective in terms of both theory and application. They have been equally successful in demonstrating that our past verbal commitment to some rehabilitative ideal has masked a set of everyday policies and practices which are unacceptably capricious and discriminatory. Their own recommendations for change, however, have proven to be largely impotent. Initially committed to a wide and inclusive reform agenda, in actual practice justice model-based changes commonly have been narrow in their focus and conservative in their impact.

Whether for better or worse, the future of penology in America will be shaped by the outcome of the battle between these groups. Neither group has won, and neither has lost. It is too early to tell whether what we are witnessing today will have a positive outcome either for our system of justice or for the hundreds of thousands of persons who each year find themselves before our criminal courts. There are some who feel that they can see some progressive light at the end of a previously dark tunnel. These optimists believe that the demise of the traditional rehabilitative model is at hand. They feel that its death will usher in new policies that will guarantee a combination of fairness, predictability, and more meaningful access to nontraditional rehabilitative programs. There are others who contend that any such light will prove to have come from a punitively motivated, conservatively fueled locomotive whose path is being charted by those seeking to erase a century or more of humanitarian reforms and rehabilitative progress. Those adopting this pessimistic stance feel that the rehabilitative model has not been given a reasonable chance to work and that its premature rejection will do nothing more than make an already bad situation even worse.

There are also those like me who see the present shifts in sentiment and practice as having the potential to permit us to make a quantum leap forward in our quest for more enlightened and less oppressive mechanisms of social control. However, we are gravely concerned by the growing indications that we may once again reveal a societal talent for snatching defeat from the jaws of victory. Perhaps the most concise history of the transitional period in which we now find ourselves was written a century ago by Charles Dickens, when he introduced a famous novel by saying: "It was the best of times, it was the worst of times, it was the age of wisdom, it was the age of foolishness, it was the epoch of belief, it was the epoch of incredulity, it was the season of Light, it was the season of Darkness, it was the spring of hope, it was the winter of despair, we had everything before us, we had nothing before us. . . .'' Time will tell.

DISCUSSION QUESTIONS

If some fraction of criminal behavior is caused by such influences as poverty, political repression, racism, and sexism, why have we tried so hard and for so long to think of ways to rehabilitate individual offenders?

It can be argued that both the rehabilitative and justice models have had exceedingly conservative impacts on our system (the rehabilitative model by focusing attention on the individual characteristics of offenders rather than the structural conditions of society, and the justice model by its narrow focus on sentencing policies to the exclusion of many other important considerations). Is this a fair assessment? Why? Why not?

THE OUTER LIMITS OF PENOLOGY

Most of what attracted our attention earlier had to do with general issues and concerns. Now, however, we need to narrow our focus considerably. How to do what must be done presents us with some very difficult choices. For example, we could limit our attention to those types or methods of responding to offenders that touch the lives of the greatest percentage of the offender population. An obvious alternative would be to deal with those responses to which we now allocate the greatest proportion of the resources available to correctional practitioners.

These and a variety of other possible directions would need to be touched on if the intent were to provide a truly comprehensive treatment of the subject matter of penology. Our rather different objectives recommend a more limited strategy, a strategy that places particular emphasis on those responses that pose special threats either to the liberty or the ives of those who are sentenced by our courts. Ours, after all, is a political and legal system within which we claim that extraordinary efforts are made to protect the rights and liberties of individual citizens. When those rights and liberties are curtailed for some extended period of time or are terminated altogether, we have arrived at the outer limits of penology. Those outer limits should provide use with the best possible vantge point from which we can evaluate our responses to what has been defined as the most problematic categories of the offender population. Thus, in the following pages we will consider the two harshest dispositions an offender in the United States can encounter; imprisonment and capital punishment.

Regarding our growing willingess to rely on imprisonment—the number of prison inmates per 100,000 citizens in our population has never been higher than it is today, and the average sentence imposed on those inmates has been rising steadily—special attention will be devoted to the difficult problems that prisons create both for those who administer them and those who are confined to within them. What we will see, unfortunately, is that our prison system has been expected to pursue so many contradictory objectives with so few resources for such a long period of time that prisons have become little more than heavily guarded warehouses within which half a million offenders must somehow cope each day with the combined effects of fear, monotony, and despair. The multidimensional problems presented by capital punishment are at least as complex and, to those like me who have many ethical and legal reasons for strongly opposing so extreme a punishment, a source of much frustration. Problems and frustration aside, it is important that we examine the present status of capital punishment in America with the objective of determining both its present legal status and evaluating what reasonable goals of punishment executions do or do not serve.

THE AMERICAN PRISON: RHETORIC VERSUS REALITY

Were casual observers of our criminal justice system to be asked what would be most likely to happen when those convicted on serious felony charges appear before trial court judges to receive their sentences, they would almost automatically think about some type of prison sentence. This image, as we have seen earlier, is not valid. The vast majority of those who find themselves awaiting the sentencing decision of trial court judges will receive a less intrusive disposition of their cases. They will pay fines, be required to make restitution to their victims, be placed on some type of probation supervision, "voluntarily" involve themselves in various types of treatment programs (e.g., drug and alcohol treatment programs), or in some other fashion be permitted to escape a harsher disposition. Prison sentences, by and large, are reserved for the fraction of offenders who have committed what are perceived to be especially serious offenses (definitions of seriousness, of course, vary from judge to judge, jurisdiction to jurisdiction, and so on) and/or who have what are perceived to be serious prior offense records. Reality aside, the fact remains that most of us think of prisons as a major means by which we go about the business of pursuing the various goals assigned to those working withn our penal system.

But what would happen if we were to push either the casual or the better informed observers for additional information? What would they be likely to say if, having been told that a given offender was to receive a prison sentence, they were aked to explain why that sentence was going to be imposed? In their responses to such a question we would quickly find one reason—perhaps even the most fundamental reason—that our use of prisons over at least the past 200 years has consistently been such an abject failure. Some would see imprisonment primarily as just punishment for past unlawful conduct. Others would see it as an important means of both deterring crime and incapacitating offenders who would posᴄ a serious threat to others were they to remain free. Still others would emphasize the importance of efforts to reform or rehabilitate. Much too often such observers would see no contradiction whatsoever in regarding all of these goals as falling within the scope of what can and should be pursued by correctional practitioners.

The bottom line, of course, is that those correctional practitioners quickly find themselves pushed into a position where they find themselves being asked to pursue fundamentally contrary objectives with a resource base that undermines their ability to do much of anything. In the abbreviated discussion that follows I review some basic information about the nearly impossible situation that correctional practitioners are now encountering and how what they do—and fail to do—plays a major role in shaping the present as well as the future attitudes, values, and behavior of offenders who are required to "do time."

Prisons as "People Processing" Organizations

There is really no simple weay to begin our discussion of prisons. It is useful, however, to remember that they are a very special type of organization in the sense that they were designed to accept human beings as their only "raw material" and to produce human beings as their only "final product." Brim and Wheeler (1966) describe such institutions as "people-processing organizations." Implicit if not explicit in such a classification is the notion that those responsible for such organizations will do something with, to, or for their raw material that will transform those who enter in some more or less planned fashion. The raw material and the final product, in other words, are intended to be two very different things.

This image of the role of prisons seems accurate enough. With the possible exception of those who view prisons as nothing more than a means of pursuing the goal of vengeance, most think of prisons as a potential instrument of change. Some, of course, think of change as nothing more than a secondary objective that must not be permitted to interfere with the business of "doing justice" (i.e., retributivists). Others think of change as the primary objective (e.g., utilitarians committed to the goalof specific deterrence and, of course, those favoring the rehabilitative model).

Given this primary or secondary emphasis on producing change, prisons can be thought of as having something in common with a host of other people-processing organizations (e.g., mental hospitals, public schools, universities, military training camps, convents, and so on). They also quality as illustrations of that very special subset of people-processing organizations that Goffman (1961b: xiii) refers to as *total institutions*. He defines total institutions as "a place of residence and work where a large number of like-situated individuals, cut off from the wider society for an appreciable period of time, together lead an enclosed, formally administered round of life." Indeed, Goffman (1961b: 5), in differentiating the five general categories of total institutions that attracted his attention, points to jails and penitentiaries (and also to POW and concentration camps) as being distinctive in that they are all "organized to protect the community against what are felt to be intentional dangers to it, with the welfare of the persons thus sequestered not the immediate issue."

Goffman, I think, was correct in his view that prisons must be seen as a special type of total institution because of the negative assessment that is made of those over whom they have been given control and because the welfare of those persons is so seldom the primary concern. His concise distinction, however, requires some extention and elaboration if we are to develop a sufficiently complete image of the organizational character of our prisons. At last three organizational features or problems warrant special emphasis: (1) *the problem of social control*, (2) *the problem of technology*, and (3) *the problem of autonomy*.

The Problem of Social Control

Perhaps the most obvious single feature of the prison in its role as a formal organization that distinguishes it from virtually all other types of people-processing organizations is the extent to which gaining and then maintaining adequate social control over its "raw material" is a persistent problem, one that consumes an inordinate fraction of its available resources (e.g., Thomas and Petersen, 1977). Social control, of course, presents a fundamental organizational problem within all organizations. No organization can hope to achieve any of the goals for which it was created unless and until those working within it (e.g., employees) and, in the special case of people-processing organizations, those who constitute its raw material (e.g., students, patients, military trainees, inmates, and so on) can be persuaded to abide by some minimal number of rules and regulations. In the absence of such a minimal level of compliance, there can be nothing other than chaos or, as one often finds in prisons, well-organized opposition to the policies and programs that prison administrators have created (e.g., Etzioni, 1975).

The problem of social control is acute in prisons for numerous reasons. To begin with, most nonprison organizations can afford to be relatively concerned with the issue of social control. There are several causes of their good fortune. First, those who enter most organizations in one capacity or another exercise some selectivity in the choices they make. Students, for instance, have some understanding of the rules, regulations, and policies of colleges and universities prior to the time at which they file admissions applications. Some of those colleges and universities place few or no constraints on their students in non-academic areas (e.g., whether they must live on campus, whether they are permitted to have cars, whether they can create and join social organizations like sororities and fraternities, whether they can consume alcoholic beverages, whether they must attend religious services, and so on). Other colleges and universities have strict regulations about these and many other things. In effect, students more or less knowingly accept or reject such policies by virtue of their decision to apply to a given school. Thus, many potential problems of control for colleges and universities are diminished greatly by the selectivity that is exercised by prospective students.

Second, of course, most organizations are able to lessen control problems by their own involvement in the selection of prospective members of their organizations. They screen applicants and reject those who are perceived to be unwilling and/or unable to meet the minimum standards set by the organization. If, to pursue the college and university illustration used before, the applicant has been suspended from another institution for disciplinary reasons, that applicant is likely to be rejected by any other college or university that has standards comparable to those the applicant has violated elsewhere.

In each of these ways, therefore, social control problems have been kept to a minimum even before prospective students have become actual students. The same is true, of course, in virtually all other types of organizations. But the relatively minimal problems most organizations have in gaining and maintaining social control cannot be explained fully by some combination of self-selection and organizational selection. Similar mechanisms remain available after someone has entered most types of organizations. The student, for instance, who discovers that the expectations of a college or university place unacceptable constraints on him or her is free to seek admission to a different institution. By the same logic, should the college or university determine that the student is not meeting its minimum standards and expectations, it can exercise whatever removal standards it has created.

In effect, then, most organizations can rely on several formal and informal means of minimizing the problems they have with social control and, consequently, the fraction of their resource bases that must be devoted to that one critically important organizational goal. The plight of prisons (and other types of organizations such as mental hospitals, POW camps, and a handful of others) in this regard should be obvious. Inmates can hardly be thought of as persons who applied for admission. Similarly, it is hard to imagine a group of prison administrators gathering together as an admissions committee and carefully sorting through a pile of folders from which they hope to select only the most promising candidates.

"Pre-entry" means of minimizing social control problems aside, "post-entry" mechanisms are in equally short supply. The "take this job and shove it, I'm not working here anymore" option is obviously not available to prison inmates who decide that they would rather take their business elsewhere. Furthermore, what do prison administrators do when they encounter inmates who refuse to comply with prison regulations? Much as inmates would welcome being fired, the option does not really exist. True, the prison administrator might be able to transfer a particular inmate from, for example, a minimum security to a medium security or a medium security to a maximum security facility. This can be and is routinely used as a control mechanism. Within a given prison system, however, things tend to work backward in comparison with other types of organizations. The best inmates are often the ones who are released rather than retained by prison organizations, while the worst inmates are typically retained for the longest periods of time.

Those responsible for people-processing as well as other types of organizations have long recognized the importance of achieving minimum levels of social control by means of techniques other than how they bring new people into their organizations and how they remove those who do not meet their expectations. Indeed, so much has been written about this topic that there is an entire body of literature on what is most commonly referred to as *compliance theory* (i.e., theoretical work about how organizations use the various powers they can rely on in their effort to bring about compliance with their rules and regulations; e.g., Etzioni, 1975). Three basic types of power have been examined fairly extensively: *normative power, remunerative power,* and *coercive power* (Etzioni, 1975: 3-22). Essentially, normative power involves the manipulation of symbolic rewards that are valued by the members of an organization (e.g., job titles, the placement and size of employee work spaces, grades assigned to students, and so on), remunerative power involves more tangible and broadly recognized rewards (especially, as the term implies, things like salaries and wages), and coercive power involves the ability of the organization to use force (e.g., placing inmates in solitary confinement, forced participation in work projects, and the like). Each of these types of power tends to foster a different type of involvement in or commitment to an organization. Normative power, in the language of compliance theory, tends to produce *moral involvement* (i.e., an intensely positive commitment to the organization), remunerative power tends to produce *calculative involvement* (i.e., neither an intensely positive nor an intensely negative commitment to the organization), and coercive power tends to produce *alienative involvement* (i.e., an intensely negative reaction to the organization).

The jargon of compliance theory aside, one of its central hypotheses is that most organizations can and do find a type of power that permits them to achieve the objective of social control. They may often do so, however, at a substantial cost in terms of their ability to pursue other organizational goals. In the case of prisons, for instance, we find a clear example of an organization that relies primarily on coerceive power as its control mechanism. On a verbal level, at least, prisons also claim that they are in the business of correcting and rehabilitating. Unfortunately, the use of coercive power and the claimed objective of change are contradictory. Change presupposes the willing (if not enthusiastic) involvement of those who are the objects of change in the change process; coercive power tends to push them in precisely the opposite direction (e.g., Thomas and Poole, 1975; Thomas, 1977). Indeed, because of the negativism and hostility one so commonly finds associated with the alienative involvement of those kept within organizations like prisons, which rely heavily or exclusively on coercive power, the very efforts prison officials make in their quest for custodial control are themselves a prime producer of control problems.

The effect of all this, of course, is that much if not most of what goes on within the context of prisons involves a constant and often counterproductive struggle to maintain control over inmate populations. This is not necessarily or even typically a consequence of prison administrators wanting to give more of a priority to the goal of maintaining custodial control rather than, for example, trying to design training or treatment programs. It is instead the almost inevitable effect of the special problems that this type of organization routinely encounters.

The Problem of Technology

Technology may seem to be a strange term when dealing with prisons or, for that matter, any other type of people-processing organization. Nevertheless, I use it to refer to the relative sophistication of the processes, procedures, and programs on which people-processing organizations rely in their efforts to transform their human raw material into something akin to a finished organizational product. It has to do, in effect, with the knowledge base on which we can draw and with how well or poorly that knowledge base permits us to achieve the goals we set out to achieve. Books like this one, theoretically at least, are part of the technology base of one type of people-processing organization. Various kinds of drugs, surgical procedures, and psychiatric or psychological strategies are part of the technology base of mental hospitals and some prisons.

The obvious problem confronted by virtually all people-processing organizations, of course, is that their processing technologies are exceedingly crude and often ineffective. Changing people—treating them, educating them, training them—has proven to be a vastly more difficult job than some may have once believed. Think, for instance, of such presumably sophisticated people-processing organizations as colleges and universities. Here and there, of course, one does encounter bits and pieces of sophisticated technology. The growing reliance on microcomputers for instructional as well as research purposes is perhaps the clearest illustration of this reality. By and large, however, the faculty and students who lived hundreds of years ago would have relatively little difficulty were they to rematerialize in the lecture halls of the "modern" university. The technology is pretty much the same today as it was in their day.

If we have learned anything about the business of people processing, it is that the body of knowledge has two common denominators: (1) Change is most probable when the objects of change are voluntarily involved in the change process and (2) change is most probable when the type of change desired can be defined in specific terms. For example, a person who is highly motivated to learn a specific skill (e.g., an academic skill like reading or mathematics, a vocational skill like repairing an automobile engine or plumbing, and so on) can be converted from raw material into a finished product fairly easily. However, if those to be changed become involuntarily involved in the change process, or if they are to be changed in relatively general rather than highly specific ways, we may encounter major problems. The worst of all possible worlds, of course, confronts those who are asked to change those who actively resist their efforts, and when the object of such change efforts is quite broad and general. Thus, the correctional practitioner who is asked to transform a hostile offender who is forced to become an inmate into someone with broadly different and also vaguely defined attitudes, values, and behavioral preferences is to ask that practitioner to do what most of us view as the impossible.

The Problem of Autonomy

Organizational theorists approach the problem of defining organizations in a variety of ways, but all of them emphasize the fact that organizations are "deliberately constructed and reconstructed to seek specific goals" (Etzioni, 1964). Such deliberate constructions include fairly complex divisions of labor within a given organization, clearly defined allocations of decision-making powers, systematic means of measuring the extent to which organizational objectives are being achieved, and a substantial capacity to redesign any or all organizational arrangements if doing so would make the organization more efficient and effective.

These and other features of a typical organization clearly presuppose that the senior executives working within and on behalf of such an organization have a considerable amount of autonomy. Based largely if not entirely on their exercise of the broad discretionary powers that have been vested in the positions they hold, people are hired and fired, priorities are established and modified, nonhuman resources (e.g., funds, space, equipment, and so on) are allocated, goals are established, and measures of efficiency and effectiveness are used to determine when or if adjustments in organizational arrangements are necessary. True, no organization is an entirely independent creature. Demand for a given product or service may grow rapidly or disappear altogether for reasons over which the organization has no control. Competing organizations may emerge than can provide a higher quality product or service, orthat can provide the same product or service at a lower cost. Economic cycles such as those that shape such factors as interest rates and the costs of raw materials are generally not subject to organizational manipulation. Overall, however, one of the defining attributes of an organization is the autonomy and control it has over its methods of operation and the goals it deems worthy of pursuit.

Here again, of course, is an area where prisons operate at a distinct disadvantage. They are a special type of what Blau and Scott (1962: 54) once referred to as *commonweal organizations:* "The distinctive characteristic of commonweal organizations is that the public-at-large is their prime beneficiary, often, although not necessarily, to the exclusion of the very people who are the object of the organization's endeavor." Especially in a democratic society, commonweal organizations confront a major challenge. On the one hand, they are expected to be as efficient and effective with regard to the puruit of their goals as other types of organizations. On the other hand, they enjoy little of the independence one typically finds in other organizational contexts: They do not set their own goals; they do not crete or have full control over their own resources; and recruitment, retention, and removal standards for employees are commonly established by persons outside the organization.

The consequences of this situation can be and often are disastrous for correctional administrators. When, for example, the popularity of some versions of the justice model began to grow a decade or so ago, politicians in the legislative bodies in dozens of states began to make major revisions in the sentencing provisions of their states' bodies of criminal law. Everyone involved either did know or should have known that those alterations would have a major effect on the size of prison population. Little thought and few computations were required. Even less thought and fewer computations were required to show that many states had no place to put the increased number of persons sentenced to a term of imprisonment. As usual, however, the politicians revealed the infrequency with which they give careful consideration to the ramifications and "ripple effects" of the legislation they approve. The certainty that the legislation they approved would require a rapid growth in prison facilities was largely ignored. (Citizens, after all, prefer to vote for politicians who are "tough on crime" but not for those who divert scarce tax revenues for costly prison construction programs.)

Today-as we find ourselves in the midst of a series of violent disturbances in our prisons and a growing number of state and federal court decisions which have defined entire prison systems as being such cruel and unusual places of punishment that they are described as being unconstitutional—we are learning that harsh sentencing policies have produced an intolerable burden on our prisons. At the end of 1984, for example, American prisons were operating at significantly more than 100 percent of their maximum population capacities, and substantially more than 11,000 offenders were being housed in local jails because the prisons in at least 18 states could find no place to put them (Bureau of Justice Statistics, 1985a). And who takes the heat? The public that continues its love affair with harsh sentences for offenders? No. The politicians who pander to that public sentiment? No. Somehow we seem fully able to lay the blame at the doorstep of those who run our prison systems. How, we ask, can those brutal people treat offenders in such a shabby way? The mindlessness of it all is amazing. The problems that come to organizations that enjoy little autonomy, however, should be obvious.

Overall, then the role of prisons as people-processing organizations continues to be very limited. Social control has long been such a persistent problem that prisons have come to define it as their primary objective rather than, as is the case in almost all other organizations, as a minimum objective which must be achieved in order to facilitate the pursuit of other more significant goals. What was to be a means to an end, in other words, became transformed into an end in and of itself. This fixation on social control has been aggravated even further by what I have described as shortcomings in the area of technology. Lacking a "people-processing technology" capable of efficiently and effectively transforming the raw material of the prison into a polished final product—indeed, lacking more than a vague notion of what that final product ought to be—prison officials have come to think of their ability to maintain control over inmate populations as providing a reasonable way of evaluating their efforts. A good job presumably has been done when physical assaults, sexual assaults, escapes, riots, and other indicators of these types are at low levels. Of course, more than a little of this must be credited to persons other than correctional administrators. Those practitioners do not set their own goals or create their own resources. They are public organizations. They enjoy relatively little organizational autonomy. Thus they do little more and little less than what the public expects and demands. Because we expect little and demand less, we get roughly what we deserve.

"Doing Time"

Those who work within our prisons are certainly not the only people within the walls of those institutions who have problems. The hundreds of thousands of inmates who are presently "doing time" would gleefully trade positions with their keepers were the opportunity to present itself. Their plight and their problems, however, are exceedingly difficult to describe in the few paragraphs that are available here. Even more detailed treatments of the issue are predestined to fall short of the mark (e.g., Sykes, 1966; Irwin, 1970, 1980; Thomas and Petersen, 1977; Toch, 1977).

Part of the difficulty, of course, is that there are such vast differences between the hundreds of prisons that are scattered across this country. Some of them, including all of the major facilities in the state where I live (Florida), are so totally oppressive that walking through their gates is a step into a chamber of horrors that is beyond anything that a human being can reasonably be asked to endure. Others, like some of the smaller and highly publicized federal facilities that are used to confine low-risk (and often well-connected) offenders require little more from offenders than a temporary deprivation of their liberty and the opportunities they would have pursued had that deprivation not been imposed on them.

Another part of the difficulty is more personal than organizational. I am reminded of a couple of lines in John Milton's epic poem, *Paradise Lost*, that go like this:

> The mind is its own place, and in itself
> Can make a heav'n of hell, a hell of heav'n.

The thought applies well to inmate responses to imprisonment. I have watched men (and women and juveniles of both sexes) respond so differently to what seemed to me to be the same objective kinds of circumstances that I long ago moved away from any of the sociology-based assertions that human behavior is thoroughly shaped by the structural conditions in which we find ourselves.

Organizational and individual differences notwithstanding, there are many problems associated with doing time in prison that have short- and long-term consequences for offender populations. At least two warrant some passing attention here: (1) problems associated with earlier phases of the criminal justice process and (2) problems associated with the status of being an inmate.

The Influence of Moving through the Criminal Justice System

It may seem strange to point to preconfinement experiences within the criminal justice system as one of the problem that have short- and long-term impacts on inmate attitudes, values, and behavior. Penologists and correctional practitioners, however, have long agreed on the powerful influence that those experiences can and do have. One can categorize such experiences in a variety of ways, but a rough distinction between those that shape assessments of equity and assessments of self are sufficient for our purposes here.

By assessments of equity, I mean the sum total of an offender's experiences within the criminal justice system but prior to his or her present confinement which shape perceptions of whether that system is just or unjust, equitable or inequitable, even-handed or discriminatory. As offenders move through the criminal justice process, regardless of whether it is a novel experience or one that they have had many times before, that experience quickly ceases to be an isolated personal event and is forced into a comparative context. At any point in time and in virtually and jurisdiction, many other cases are being processed. Those cases may be very similar to or quite different from that of a particular offender. It is only natural that each offender will develop (accurately or inaccurately) some rough assessment of whether his or her case is being handled in a manner akin to that accorded what he or she sees as being comparable cases and, of course, an interpretation of what produced any similarities or differences.

An artificial illustrtion should be sufficient to make the point. Assume that Joe, a young black male who had been working as an unskilled construction laborer, was charged with burglary and grand theft after he broke into a sporting goods store and stole $5000 worth of firearms. Unable to come up with the money to obtain a release on bail, he was confined in a crowded city jail for several months before his trial. While awaiting trial, he read a newspaper story about a computer programmer who, while employed by a large local bank, had successfully executed a sophisticated scheme that permitted him to steal more than a million dollars from several corporate bank accounts. While none of the money had been recovered, bank officials and the chief prosecutor in the city had agreed that no criminal charges would be filed if the computer programmer revealed the specific details of how he had stolen such a large amount of money so that the bank officials, in turn, could take steps to prevent any such offenses in the future. Soon thereafter the ex-construction worker, despite the fact that he had no prior criminal record and had cooperated with the court and prosectuor by entering a plea of guilty to both charges, received a sentence of 15 years in the state penitentiary with no possibility of early release on parole until at least five years of the sentence had been served. On his arrival at the state's central inmate classification center, the responsibility of which includes determining whether offenders should be assigned to a minimum, medium or maximum security facility, classification personnel quickly observed that Joe was hostile, uncooperative, and, they suspected, potentially violent. He was promptly transferred to a maximum security prison.

If the hypothetical case of Joe is similar to that of tens of thousands of others who move through our criminal justice system each year, a significant portion of his initial response to confinement must be related to his reaction to how his case was handled relative to the treatment accorded others. In the midst of all of the wheeling and dealing and bargaining that takes place within our criminal justice system, a substantial number of offenders come to think of their treatment as being analogous either to a lottery which permits the lucky to be treated very leniently or to the outcome of conscious discrimination based on an improper consideration of such variables as race, sex, socioeconomic status, and political power (e.g., Thomas and Hepburn, 1983: 500-538). Both perceptions foster feelings of unfairness and inequity, and those feelings in turn promote high levels of alienation, hostility, and negativism among those who enter our prison systems.

Moving through the criminal justice system shapes self-assessments as well as assessments of equity. Experiences associated with being arrested, jailed, charged, placed on trial, and convicted can hardly be described as positive. Whether intentionally or unintentionally, they have a dramatic effect on our perceptions of those who encounter such experiences and on the self-perceptions of those who are processed. Suddenly people who were once evaluated on the basis of many of their social and personal characteristics—whether they are black or white, male or female, rich or poor, married or unmarried, employed or unemployed, and so on—are evaluated by others (and often by themselves) primarily on the basis of negative labels attached to them by the criminal justice system. The assault on conceptions of self and self-worth is often considerable (e.g., McCorkle and Korn, 1954; Cloward, 1960; Goffman, 1961; Bowker, 1977). Indeed, as Cloward (1960: 21) aptly observed many years ago, "the inmate social system may be viewed as providing a way of life which enables the inmate to avoid the devastating psychological effects of internalizing and converting social rejection into self-rejection."

Becoming a Prison Inmate

Notwithstanding the significance that must be attached to those preconfinement experiences that shape perceptions of equity and self, becoming an inmate involves a broad spectrum problems that are specific to the prison itself. These problems have been described and categorized in many different ways (e.g., Sykes, 1966; Toch, 1977; Thomas and Hepburn, 1983). Regardless of how they are described, the objective is to reveal the major deprivations to which inmates must adapt either as individuals or as a group. Elsewhere (Thomas and Hepburn, 1983: 503), I have suggested that most of the major problems and deprivations fall into one of four more or less separate categories: "(1) the degradation rituals associated with entry into the prison, (2) the problems of prison life itself, (3) the disruption of relationships beyond the walls of the prison, and (4) the anxieties linked to forthcoming release from prison." Here, however, I deal primarily with the first two of these categories.

First of all, partly because they tend to be organizations which are called upon to deal with large number of people and partly because of the negative assessments that have been made of those who are committed to them, prisons rely on what have been referred to as "degradation rituals" (Garfinkel, 1956; Goffman, 1961). The objective, whether carefully conceived or partly accidental, is to strip offenders of whatever identity they may have had in the "free world" and to substitute a new and very different identity. Such processes are not unknown in nonprison contexts. Induction processes relied on by such diverse groups as social clubs, fraternities and sororities, the military, some colleges and universities (esecially the various military academies), and some religious orders are quite similar in many important regards. In prisons as well as other settings, the intent is clear. "New recruits" are to be transformed from a set of separate individuals who have equally separate and distinct identities into a far more homogeneous group of people who come to see that what they share in common—their new status—is the most important means by which they are defined by others and by themselves. In most roughly analogous contexts, of course, the new status is believed to be positive, something to be valued. In the prison context, however, these degradation or induction rituals are aimed at convincing new offenders that they are negatively evaluated outcasts from the larger society who will now occupy powerless positions at the very bottom of the organizational structure of the prison.

Second, however assaultive induction or degradation rituals may be on the physical and psychological well-being of newly arrived inmates, "arrival problems" quickly give way to problems associated with everyday prison life. Sykes (1966), for example, describes the "pains of imprisonment" as involving such important deprivations as those associated with the loss of liberty, autonomy, security, heterosexual relationships, and the sorts of goods and services that are readily available outside of the prison. He is certainly correct. Trying to adapt to life in prison is difficult even for those who have done time in the past. The predictability of daily schedules is so great that the sheer monotony of life becomes a major problem. The endless noise and clamor of hundreds if not thousands of inmates jammed into a small amount of space has always grated on my nerves—and I have enjoyed the freedom to walk out whenever I felt like doing so. Access to even the most mundane degrees of personal privacy quickly becomes a hazy memory. The threat of violence is never far away. The risk of trusting virtually anyone with regard to almost anything can never be ignored. Prison food—while sometimes not as bad as you might expect—is at best so blandly institutional in character that it only aggravates the monotony and routine that none can escape for long. These and dozens of other problems create an atmosphere that is never far from being explosive. Tiny and objectively trivial events—an accidental bumping of one inmate by another, the expected arrival of a visitor who never appears, news about problems being experienced by a spouse or child, the cancellation of a scheduled bit of entertainment, the serving of an especially unappealing meal, the changing of a television channel, an unanticipated cell search, an unusually hot and humid day—can produce explosive consequences.

Space does not permit a thorough discussion of the role played by these and other problems of confinement, but care should be taken to understand one important common denominator: In most of the settings in which we find ourselves, we either can, or believe we can, take some action that will permit us to adapt to or escape from the problems we confront. Ture, our perceptions of control are often illusions. For example, I have often said that if I really come to dislike my role as a university professor, I would resign and become a ful-time studio potter. There was even a time when I considered pursuing that option. Most of us have that sort of mental image of freedom, but the very remote likelihood of the mental image becoming reality does not dull the ability of the image to make us feel that we have substantial control over our lives. The world is not the same for prison inmates. Time after time and day after day, they are reminded that they are individually powerless to shape the course of their own lives. Individually, they are impotent. They are isolated. They are subordinate. They are dependent. They are the objects rather than the holders of power. If they have influence or power to control significant aspects of everyday life, then that influence and power must come from them as members of a group rather than as individual people.

The Inmate Society

Perhaps some of what has been said has left the impression that those who operate our prison system exercise so much coercive power other those who are doing time that each and every feature of the everyday lives of inmates is shaped by prison officials. While this is true in some ways, it is often more realistic to think of prison officials as the persons who maintain the boundaries of the prison and as inmates as the persons who (directly or indirectly) control virtually everything else.

Much the same is true, of course, in other types of people-processing organizations. Think again, for instance, of colleges and universities. While administrators and faculty have much control over some aspects of student life and some control over many others, over the years a remarkable amount of power has either been formally delegated to or informally assumed by students. Traditions develop over time to which considerable influence is attached. The peculiar features and problems associated with student life contribute to the development of a sometimes strange vocabulary that is largely unique to the campus. Informal as well as formal socialization processes emerge in the hope that newly arrived students can acquire what are perceived to be more appropriate attitudes, values, vocabularies, appearances, and so on. Consequently, whether being a student is easy or hard, enjoyable or frustrating, or associated with increases or decreases in self-esteem comes to depend in large measure on the degree to which new arrivals assimilate into the society of students.

All of this, of course, can be observed in a variety of other contexts (e.g., basic training camps for military recruits, religious institutions like monasteries, high schools, and so on). What people were in the past interacts with what people confront in the present—and the present always involves more than our membership in a single organization—as well as with what they anticipate in the future. Naturally, the ability of any of these more or less independent influences to shape how we feel, think, and behave at a given point in time is not constant from person to person, day to day, or organization to organization.

Once again, ignore the probably unfamiliar role of being an inmate and consider the more familiar role of being a student. The influence exerted by students' past experiences tends to diminish over time as those past experiences become more and more a part of students' life histories. The influence of present involvements in campus life increases as the distance between previous roles and graduation dates reach a maximum level. It is no accident that college sophomores are so often used as examples of both the best and the worst of what students cn be. The influence of present involvements also increases when they bring high levels of stress and pressure (e.g., examination week). But the outside world is seldom altogether irrelevant. Positive events (e.g., approaching vacations, the marriage of a close relative, and so on) and negative events (e.g., the illness or death of a family member) can reduce substantially the relevance of whatever student status may involve. Similarly, anticipations regarding the future frequently intrude to elevate or diminish campus-specific influences. The need many students feel to maintain high grade point averages so that they will be qualified to enter graduate or professional schools is an obvious illustration of this reality.

Understand that none of the above comments are intended to provide a short course on colleges and universities in their capacities as people-processing organizations, and I am certainly not suggesting that prisons and institutions of higher education are equivalent organizational forms. What I am saying is that all too often we approach the study of prisons and of the inmate society as though we were examining some totally alien life forms that just arrived from another galaxy. That is a foolish mistake. Prisons are nothing more or less than a special kind of organization that approaches a special kind of task and deals with a special kind of raw material. They are, to be more specific, total institutions that by choice and/or necessity have come to rely on very high levels of coercive power with the primary objective of maintaining custodial control over large numbers of offenders who, by and large, are poorly educated, largely lacking in the professional or vocational skills required to survive in conventional society, experienced in their dealings with the criminal justice system, and in various other ways disproportionately representative of the most disadvantaged categories of our population. Most of life in the inmate society is nothing more or less than a predictable outcome of influences that are directly associated with what prisons share in common with a host of other people-processing institutions in addition to the relatively unique influences that attach to the special type of organization that prisons represent.

What, then, is the inmate society? What does participation in it involve? What are the consequences of those involvements? By now it should be clear that there is no one answer for any of these questions. Not all prisons are alike. They vary significantly in, for instance, their size, the quality of their physical facilities, the sophistication of their employees, the characteristics of their inmate populations, and the degree to which they are able or willing to move beyond pursuing goals other than control. These organizational differences have consistently been shown to have a major effect on the character and consequences of involvements in the inmate society (e.g., Grusky, 1959; Street et al., 1966; Berk, 1966; Akers et al., 1977; Goodstein, 1979; Moczydlowski, 1983). Generally speaking, however, the vast majority of criminologists have concentrated their attention on explaining the origins and assessing the effects of involvement in the typical type of inmate society that they believe may produce rather than prevent crime. The central features of the normative system in such contexts has been described by Ohlin (1956: 28-29):

> The [inmate] code represents an organization of criminal values in clear-cut opposition to the values of conventional society, and to prison officials as representatives of that society. The main tenet of this code forbids any type of supportive or nonexploitative liaison with prison officials. It seeks to confer status and prestige on those inmates who stand most clearly in opposition to the administration. . . . These criminal beliefs and attitudes place a high premium on physical violence and strength, on exploitative sex relations, and predatory attitudes toward money and property. They place a strong emphasis on in-group loyalty and solidarity and on aggressive and exploitative relations with conventionally oriented out-groups.

Studies of the inmate society and the inmate code—its characteristics, the influences that result in its acceptance, and its consequences on the postrelease attitudes, values, and behavior of inmates—date back for more than a half century and now number in the hundreds. The space available here precludes anything more than a superficial set of comments (but for a fairly thorough overview, see Bowker, 1977). Reduced to a bare-bone summary, researchers have concentrated their attention on two dependent variables: *prisonization* and *inmate social roles*. Prisonization is a term that was first used by Clemmer in his *The Prison Community* (1940) and that he later defined as "the taking on in greater or less degree of the folkways, mores, customs, and general culture of the penitentiary" (Clemmer, 1958: 299). The term refers, in effect, to a socialization or an assimilative process by means of which new inmates learn and come to accept the attitudes, values, and norms of the inmate society. Interest in inmate social roles also has a lengthy history in criminological research (e.g., Schrag, 1944, 1961). These roles reflect the types of positions that inmates come to occupy within the informal structure of inmate societies (e.g., Irwin and Cressey, 1962; Garabedian, 1963; Giallombardo, 1966; Glaser, 1964; Thomas and Foster 1972, 1973; Poole et al., 1980). These positions can be examined at a fairly low level of abstraction—as with a variety of research on the economic, sexual, and political behavior of particular categories of inmates—or at a general level of analysis, as with the work of criminologists like Schrag (1961: 348-350), who discusses what he refers to as asocial, prosocial, antisocial, and pseudosocial role adaptations.

While this literature is far too large and diverse to permit the construction of precise categories, it is probably accurate to say that the bulk of it can be linked to efforts to develop or test one of two fairly crude theoretical points of view. One of these is commonly referred to as the *deprivation model*. The other has been labeled the *importation model*. These perspectives differ primarily in the extent to which they view the immediate problems of adaptation to life in prison as the major force that shapes inmate attitudes, values, behavior, and—perhaps—their postrelease behavior. Early statements of the deprivation model certainly leave one with the impression that the various problems of adaptation that all inmates confront are the dominant forces which shape the nature of the inmate society and the normative content of the inmate code (e.g., Sykes and Messinger, 1960; Goffman, 1961). Those who have worked with the importation model, while recognizing many of the same variables identified by the deprivation model, emphasize that much of what takes place within the walls of the prison reflects the effects of a variety of attitudes and behavior patterns that had been established prior to the point of inmates having been confined (e.g., Clemmer, 1958; Irwin and Cressey, 1962; Carroll, 1974; Thomas and Cage, 1977; Jacobs, 1977, 1979).

Suffice it to say that criminologists today generally agree that neither the deprivation model nor the important model provides an adequate explanation for what we see taking place within the context of the inmate society. Most if not all now accept the need to merge these two perspectives into one broader and more inclusive theory (e.g., Wellford, 1967; Thomas, 1970, 1977; Schwartz, 1971; Akers, 1977). Prison violence, for instance, cannot be understood fully simply by examining the levels of tension, anxiety, and pressure of life within a particular prison. Important though such variables may be, it is also true that much prison violence is the consequence of group or gang memberships that offenders had prior to their being confined and of the racial and political tensions they experienced in the larger society (e.g., Carroll, 1974; Jacobs, 1977). Similarly, the high levels of homosexuality that have been reported in so many studies of inmate populations might at first appear to be little more than an obvious adaptation toward which inmates are driven by the deprivation of heterosexual outlets that characterize most, though not all, prisons. On closer inspection, however, we find that sexual behavior within the prison has many important ties to a combination of the problems presented by life in prison and by life experiences prior to confinement (e.g., Giallombardo, 1966; Heffernan, 1972; Carroll, 1974).

The Consequences of Confinement

After decades of work and the publication of hundreds of relevant papers, articles, and monographs, there is a paradox in this area of penology that must not go unmentioned. On the one hand, our body of theory and research has improved significantly. We are now in a far better position to understand how a host of variables shape the adaptations and reactions of inmates than we ever enjoyed before. On the other hand, much of the effort has been expended because of the belief that prison experiences often increase rather than decrease the likelihood of criminal behavior among those who are returned to the larger society. It has often been argued, for example, that high levels of prisonization and the assumption of other than prosocial inmate social roles is likely to increase the likelihood of recidivism. Today, however, the direct effect of prison adaptations and experiences on postrelease behavior is anything but clear. Indeed, a growing body of evidence points to the possibility that variables like prisonization and social role adaptations have at most a very modest relationship with how offenders relate to the free society after release from prison (e.g., Glaser, 1964; Kassenbaum et al., 1971; Goodstein, 1979). To the extent that this is true, those who are concerned with findings which reveal that one-half to two-thirds of all released inmates are likely to recidivate will have to shift their attention from what goes on within our prisons to the many obstacles that limit the ability of many offenders to make a smooth transition from the role of inmate to the very difficult role of ex-convict.

THE DEATH PENALTY IN AMERICA

While we are nearly at the end of the space available for this overview of the field of penology, at least some attention must be given to the topic of capital punishment. Of all the crime-related issues that have attracted the interest of both research criminologists and the public at large, I know of none that poses so many nearly impossible moral, legal, and criminological problems. My own research on the death penalty began more than a decade ago. In the years that have followed I have encountered only two categories of people for whom the many problems have a fairly matter-of-fact resolution. One of these includes what for me is an unfortunately large number of people who see no problem. For them the world is a black or white entity within which the death penalty is perceived to be a perfectly appropriate—perhaps even the only appropriate—legal reaction to those who have committed what they take to be especially heinous criminal offenses. Such people see a victim and demand the imposition of a sentence of death. They see no problem with the particulars of how law is created, with clear evidence regarding the conviction of persons who are later proved to be innocent, with the random and sometimes discriminatory manner by means of which law is frequently applied, with the wheeling and dealing that so commonly takes place in encounters between defendants and prosecutors, with mounds of research evidence which questions the ability of the death penalty to move us toward such goals as crime deterrence, and with the whim and caprice that sometimes control the exercise of the discretionary powers our legal system vests in trial court juries, trial court judges, and appellate courts. The other groups include those whose moral, philosophical, or religious beliefs flatly define the death penalty as inappropriate and intolerable under any and all circumstances. These abolitionists share something very much like the black or white world in which the first group lives. No matter what the nature of a criminal offense might be and no matter what the characteristics of our legal system might be or be made to become, those in this second group find no defense for so extreme a punishment.

Polar groups like these can be found whenever especially troublesome issues will not go away and cannot be avoided. The examples are numerous. Should we use nuclear energy as a power source? Should we have nuclear weapons? Should any materials be defined as unlawful because they are pornographic? Should abortions be permitted? Should the use of a variety of drugs be prohibited by our criminal law? With regard to these and many other questions, it is easy to find significant numbers of people who almost instantly can give positive or negative answers. Such positions are absolutely unequivocal; they cannot be changed. Evidence of any kind is nothing more or less than something to be used in support of a previously accepted position if it "fits" or ignored altogether if it does not. Thus, the passion of commitment to chosen positions too often becomes a replacement for reliance on objectivity, reason, and sound evidence.

Most of us lack the comfort of such total confidence. Most of us lack the ability to define all who disagree with us as unfortunates who refuse to see The Light and to accept The Answer. I freely admit here that I sometimes wish that my own thoughts regarding capital punishment had given way to some simple if rigid position. It has not happened for me yet and I am but one of many who see exceedingly difficult questions and few if any precise answers. In fairness to the reader, however, I will quickly admit a very strong and negative bias toward the death penalty. I have seen no circumstance that would permit me to view an execution as the only just legal response. I have seen no reasonable evidence that executions yield any meaningful future benefits—certainly not benefits that could not be achieved were less extreme sentences to be imposed. My years of work within our criminal system have confronted me with much evidence that the system often works in a manner that is at once capricious and discriminatory. Consequently, it is my present position that the death penalty cannot reasonably be said to be the only possible deserved punishment for any particular class of offenders, that the death penalty has never been shown to be an important means by which we can go about the business of achieving any reasonable future benefits of punishment, and that our system of justice is so fundamentally unjust in its everyday operation that no representative of that system should have access to so awesome a sentencing alternative. Rightly or wrongly, however, I take these elements of my own position as being based on the best available research evidence. I hope that this means that the following very abbreviated discussion of the death penalty is something other than an ideologically based statement of my own moral or political preferences.

Our review of the death penalty in America can be best structured if we concentrate our attention on the following basic questions. First, of course, are a set of questions regarding our ability to offer a sound moral justification for the death penalty. I refer the reader back to earlier portions of our discussion, especially Chapter 2, for relevant information regarding those concerns. Second, we need to ask questions regarding the history of our reliance on the death penalty. Third, we need to examine the present legal status of capital punishment.

A Recent History of Capital Punishment in America

Because of the relative infrequency of executions in the United States during the past two decades—there were no executions between 1967 and 1977, and a historically moderate 47 executions from 1977 until when this chapter was written (August of 1985)—many younger readers may be unaware of how often executions once took place in this country. Estimates of the total volume of legal executions in the United States suggest that there have been at least 14,029 of them (e.g., Streib, 1983). Even if attention is limited to roughly the last half century, we find that 3905 persons have been executed in the United States. Indeed, throughout the 1930s and 1940s there were an average of more than two executions per week, the annual number of executions never dropped below 119 (in 1940), and the total number of executions frequently approached the 200 level several times (e.g., 199 in 1935, 195 in 1936, and 190 in 1938; Bureau of Justice Statistics, 1984c: 14). Thus, those who today view the death penalty as something of a legal antique—and also those who doubt that contemporary American society would be willing to tolerate significant numbers of executions—strike me as being flatly incorrect.

Historical data on levels of executions aside, there are several dimensions of the death penalty topic that deserve special emphasis here. First of all, the death penalty is not a sentence that we have been willing to impose with any real frequency for offenses other than those involving the unlawful taking of human lives. Taking 1930 once again as a starting point, for example, 86.56 percent of all executions have involved persons convicted of criminal homicide, 11.65 percent have involved persons convicted of rape, and only 1.79 have involved persons convicted of other crimes (i.e., 25 of armed robbery, 20 of kidnapping, 11 for burglary, 6 for sabotage, 6 for aggravated assault, and 2 for espionage; Bureau of Justice Statistics, 1984c, plus personal files on recent executions). Recent legal decisions—especially holdings of the U.S. Supreme Court in *Coker v. Georgia* (453 U.S. 584, 1977) and *Enmund v. Florida* (102 S.Ct. 3368, 1982)—make it highly unlikely that nonhomicide offenses can be responded to with sentences of death.

Second, anyone who reviews either the overall or the recent history of the death penalty in the United States will necessarily come away from his or her study of the topic with two conclusions that necessarily raise grave questions about our use of this most extreme punishment. One of these findings has to do with the tiny percentage of persons who are convicted of crimes that could result in sentences of death who actually receive such a sentence. Data on criminal homicides known to the police relative to the present death row population provide at least a crude indicator of the point I am trying to make. Over the past decade, official crime statistics show that some 215,000 persons have been murdered in this country. While a significant but unknown fraction of those criminal homicides involved offenders who were never convicted, who were convicted in jurisdictions that have abolished the death penalty, or who were convicted of types of criminal homicide for which the death penalty is not a legal possibility, certainly tens of thousands of these cases do involve persons who were convicted and who could have received a sentence of death. However, recent figures show 47 executions and a death row population of 1540 (a significant number of whom were under a sentence of death before the ten-year period being considered began).

Such an imbalance between any estimate of the number of offenders who could have received a sentence of death and those who actually did receive such a sentence could, and in some measure surely does, reflect our inclination to reserve capital punishment for those who are believed to be the most heinous offenders. Notwithstanding this fact, researchers have been unsuccessful in their efforts to identify any meaningful method of predicting which otherwise eligible offenders will or will not be sentenced to death. Thus, for example, in the landmark U.S. Supreme Court decision of *Furman v. Georgia* (408 U.S. 238, 309, 1972), Justice Stewart complained that sentences of death "are cruel and unusual in the same way that being struck by lightning is cruel and unusual. . . . [T] he petitioners are among a capriciously selected handful upon whom the sentence of death" has been imposed, and Justice White (408 U.S. 238, 313, 1972) concluded that "the death penalty is exacted with great infrequency even for the most atrocious crimes. . . . [T]here is no meaningful basis for distinguishing the cases in which it is imposed from the many cases in which it is not."

The other conclusion that cannot be escapted when the history of the death penalty is considered is that some of the variables that have been used to predict who will and will not receive a sentence of death reflect evidence of constitutionally intolerable discrimination on the basis of such influences as sex, race, and economic status (e.g., Wolfgang and Riedel, 1973; Riedel, 1976; Bowers and Pierce, 1980; Radelet, 1981; Black, 1982; Radelet and Vandiver, 1983; Bowers, 1983; Paternoster, 1984; Bentele, 1985; Endres, 1985: 31-65). Certainly the most painfully obvious illustration of this bias in the history of executions in this country came with data on persons whose executions followed their conviction on rape charges (e.g., Bureau of Justice Statistics, 1984c). For example, data on executions of children below the age of 18—and there have been 287 of these in our history— show a total of 31 executions for rape and 11 for attempted rape. All 42 offenders were black (Streib, 1983: 621). Similarly, almost 90 percent of all such executions between 1930 and today involved black offenders, most commonly black males convicted of raping white females. In six jurisdictions—Washington, D.C., Virginia, West Virginia, Mississippi, Louisiana, and Oklahoma—the record shows multiple executions of blacks convicted on rape charges but not a single execution of a white offender during that 55-year time span. The appearance of racial discrimination is nearly as obvious in many other jurisdictions. In Georgia, for example, there have been 61 executions of persons convicted of rape. Of these, 58 were black males. Similarly, in North Carolina only four of 47 executed rapists were white males.

While contemporary research on bias does not reveal such obvious evidence of discrimination on the basis of variables other than sex— only 20 of the present 1540 offenders on death row are female—the problem clearly persists. A growing body of evidence, for example, shows that the race of the victims of criminal homicide plays a significant role in shaping the likelihood that prosecutors will seek the death penalty and the likelihood that offenders will receive sentences of death (e.g., Wolfgang and Riedel, 1973; Radelet, 1981; Radelet and Pierce, 1985). Relatively recent (i.e., post-1976) adjustments in the provisions of statutory law and rules of criminal procedure increased the probability that such bias would be detected by our appellate courts. The Radelet and Vandiver (1983: 924) study of the role being played by the Florida Supreme Court, for instance, shows that "in nearly half of the Florida death penalty cases reviewed since 1972, the state supreme court has found flaws or errors of such severity that it could not affirm the penalty [of death]." However, the historical tradition of according a presumption of validity to trial court proceedings precludes us from relying on our appellate courts to correct more than a fraction of the errors that come before them.

What we see over the past half century or so, then, is a frequent reliance on the death penalty during the 1930s and 1940s, a swift reduction in the annual number of executions during the 1950s and 1960s, no executions whatsoever from 1967 until 1977 (some of the reasons for this moratorium will be reviewed in a moment), and, especially during the past year or two, a rapid rise in the number of executions. The vast majority of those who have been executed were convicted or murder or rape. Most if not all of us would define these kinds of offenses as especially serious violations of criminal law, violations that should be met with harsh punishment. Most if not all of us, however, also share the viewpoint that all punishments—most particularly those that are unusually severe or, as with the death penalty, beyond adjustment if the need for adjustment is called for by subsequent experience or evidence—should be imposed in a reasonable, fair, and impartial fashion. It is for precisely such reasons that so many are so hostile to capital punishment. Research on the death penalty consistently suggests either that it is imposed in a fashion that has more in common with a lottery than with justice or that the likelihood of its being imposed is correlated with influences that are alien to a legal system that proclaims a commitment to due process and equal protection under the law. Consequently, and quite apart from such entirely relevant factors as the value we claim to place on the inherent value of human life, simple considerations of fairness and equity make it exceedingly difficult to endorse any continued reliance on the death penalty. That something on the order of three-quarters of the adult population in this country continues to reject this conclusion strikes me more as a reflection of their understandable ignorance of the best available evidence than as a commitment on their part to endorse the *lex talionis* principle of "an eye for an eye, a tooth for a tooth." Unfortunately, I think, the growing number of persons awaiting execution in the United States stands as a stark testimonial to the fact that ignorance is not bliss. It is deadly.

The Legal and Constitutional Status of the Death Penalty

I approach commenting on the present legal and constitutional status of the death penalty with grave reservations. The relevant statutory provisions, appellate court cases, and scholarly commentaries have become so voluminous and complex that they almost defy any simple efforts at summarization. My reservations aside, there are a few fundamental points that really must be made and, with luck, I can identify some important additional materials for the interested reader.

I begin with a few introductory comments about the legal history of the death penalty in the United States. Suffice it to say that for most of our history, the legality and constitutionality of the death penalty has not been open to much debate. Indeed, early decisions of the U.S. Supreme Court regarding capital punishment focused quite narrowly on whether a particular method of execution—shooting, hanging, electrocution, and so on—was constitutional and not at all on whether the death penalty per se was defective (e.g., *Wilkerson v. Utah,* 99

U.S. 130, 1879, shooting and hanging; *Medley, Petitioner,* 134 U.S. 160, 1890, hanging; *In re Kemmler,* 136 U.S. 436, 1890, electrocution; and, though in state appellate court holdings, *State v. Gee Jon*, 211 P. 676, Nevada 1923, lethal gas; and *People v. Daughtery*, 256 P.2d 911, California 1953, *cert. denied,* 346 U.S. 827, 1953, lethal gas). Throughout this set of cases, the language and reasoning relied on by the court in *Wilkerson* repeats itself: "It is safe to affirm that punishments of torture…and all others in the same line of unnecessary cruelty, are forbidden by that amendment [the Eighth Amendment] to the Constitition"; otherwise the method of punishment is without constitutional defect. Only infrequently did the appellate courts give any consideration whatsoever to relevant features of the criminal justice process (but see *Powell v. Alabama*, 287 U.S. 45, 1932, wherein the Court held that defendants in capital cases did have a constitutionally protected right to counsel). In fact, in *Louisiana ex rel. Francis v. Resweber* (329 U.S. 459, 1947), the Supreme Court reviewed a case involving an inmate who had been sentenced to die in Louisiana. An initial attempt to electrocute him proved to be unsuccessful. The offender was shocked, but he did not die. The Court was asked to declare a second effort to electrocute the offender as a cruel and unusual punishment, but it saw no constitutional flaw in what had taken place! Equally uncommon was any appellate court attentiveness to the harshness of either sentences of death or other (relative to the gravity of noncapital crimes) offenses (for exceptions to this general rule, see *O'Neil v. Vermont*, 144 U.S. 155, 1892; *Weems v. United States,* 217 U.S. 349, 1910; *Trop v. Dulles,* 356 U.S. 86, 1958).

The willingness of the appellate courts to find fundamental constitutional defects in capital punishment statutes or the manner in which such statutes were being applied remained at a low level even when we encountered sweeping evidence of judicial activism during the 1960s (e.g., Meltsner, 1973; Bedau, 1977, 1983; King, 1982; Endres, 1985). Indeed, apart from some indications that a minority of the members of the U.S. Supreme Court were willing to entertain the hypothesis that death sentences for persons convicted of nonhomicide offenses might well constitute a cruel and unusual punishment of the type prohibited by the Eighth Amendment (e.g., *Rudolph v. Alabama,* 375 U.S. 889, 1963), the abolitionist assault on capital punishment did not really begin to bear fruit until around 1967. At and soon after that time, their position began to prevail before both the lower federal courts (e.g., *Adderly v. Wainwright,* 272 F.Supp. 530, M.D. Fla. 1967; *Hill v. Nelson*, 272 F.Supp. 790, N.D. Cal. 1967;

Ralph v. Warden, 438 F.2d 786, 4th Cir. 1970) and the U.S. Supreme Court (see especially *Witherspoon v. Illinois,* 391 U.S. 510, 1968).

By blocking the executions of any death row inmates in Florida and California, the lower court holdings set the stage for a full decade (1967-1977) during which there were no executions in the United States. *Witherspoon* and its progeny (e.g., *Adams v. Texas,* 448 U.S. 38, 1980) greatly reduced the ability of prosecutors to challenge the suitability of prospective members of juries in death penalty cases based on nothing more than their admission of opposition to capital punishment. (Prior to *Witherspoon,* prosecutors could pose questions to prospective jurors during what is called the *voir dire*—a pretrial phase at which both defense counsel and prosecutors can seek to remove prospective jurors who are believed to be biased. If those questions revealed even modest degrees of opposition to the death penalty, the prosecution would request that they be removed from the pool of potential candidates for the trial court jury. The obvious result, of course, was a "death-qualified jury." In other words, juries in death penalty cases would contain no juror who had expressed opposition to capital punishment and an entire set of people who, at least by implication, supported the use of that type of punishment.)

A growing set of issues finally came before the U.S. Supreme Court in *Furman v. Georgia* (408 U.S. 238, 1972). In this landmark, lengthy, and very complex opinion, the Court held that capital punishment was prohibited by the cruel and unusual punishment clause of the Eighth Amendment, a clause made applicable to criminal proceedings of the individual states by the due process and equal protection clause of the Fourteenth Amendment. The Court, however, was badly split on this case—five justices made up the majority, with four justice dissenting. Even those justices in the majority group disagreed with one another. Three found major procedural flaws in the death penalty statutes they reviewed. Only two reached the conclusion that the death penalty was unconstitutional without regard to the offenses for which it was made applicable or the procedures by means of which it was applied. Thus, while some of the more naive abolitionists concluded that the war had been won when the *Furman* decision was announced, most knew that they had won no more than a single battle.

History shows that the skeptics were correct. During the four years following *Furman,* dozens of states sought to draft revised death penalty statutes capable of satisfying the objections of at least five justices of the Supreme Court. Two general plans of attack quickly became apparent: *mandatory death penalty statutes* and *guided dis-*

cretion statutes. While much variation existed within these two broad categories of statutes, the mandatory approach sought to avoid problems of capriciousness and discrimination by requiring that all persons convicted of narrowly defined types of capital crimes would automatically and necessarily receive sentences of death. The guided discretion schemes sought to achieve the same objectives,m but they attempted to do so by way of statutes that provided trial court judges and juries with various types of guidelines and criteria. Both types of efforts came before the Supreme Court for review in five murder cases in 1976: *Gregg v. Georgia* (428 U.S. 153); *Proffitt v. Florida* (428 U.S. 242); *Jurek v. Texas* (428 U.S. 262); *Woodson v. North Carolina* (428 U.S. 280); and *Roberts v. Louisiana* (428 U.S. 325). Georgia, Florida, and Texas provided examples of the guided discretion approach. North Carolina and Louisiana had adopted mandatory sentencing schemes.

Suffice it to say that the court found constitutional defects in the mandatory sentencing efforts, largely because they did not provide the defendants with a right to introduce evidence regarding their personalities, backgrounds, and various information about the circumstances surrounding their offenses. Punishment, reasoned the court, has to do with much more than a determination that a defendant is guilty of a particular offense when that offense is defined as a capital crime. The guided discretion statutes, however, were found to be constitutional. For instance, they reflected an effort to channel and direct the exercise of judicial and jury discretion and to thereby avoid arbitrariness and discrimination. They also provided for what are now referred to as bifurcated trials. In these two-stage trials, the first stage is limited to a determination of guilt or innocence. If the defendant is found to be guilty, there is a "sentencing trial" during which both prosecution and defense have—especially after such subsequent holdings of the Court as *Lockett v. Ohio* (438 U.S. 586, 1978) and *Bell v. Ohio* (438 U.S. 637, 1978)—a full and fair opportunity to introduce evidence that is of relevance to whether the convicted offender deserves a sentence of death.

The post-*Gregg* era in which we now find ourselves is almost as frustrating for advocates of the death penalty as it is depressing for those who are abolitionists. Those favoring the death penalty have been successful in their efforts to encourage legislative bodies to enact death penalty statutes. In all, 37 states have such statutes. There are persons awaiting execution in no fewer than 32 states. Proponents are also pleased that efforts by abolitionists to block executions via a host of different delaying tactics have proven to be unsuccessful—47 percent have been executed since 1977. They are angered, however, by the unwillingness of the appellate courts to limit the range of postconviction strategies on which defense counsel rely, strategies that often involve a decade or more of costly litigation before sentences of death can be carried out. They are no more pleased with various Supreme Court decisions that have limited the imposition of death sentences to an increasingly narrow set of offenders. In *Coker v. Georgia* (433 U.S. 584, 1977), for example, the court held that the imposition of sentences of death for persons convicted of rape was unconstitutional because such sentneces were unacceptably harsh relative to the seriousness of the offense committed. The practical effect of *Coker*—at least thus far—has been to block the execution of any person who has not been convicted of especially serious forms of murder. Similarly, in *Enmund v. Florida* (102 S.Ct. 3368, 1982), the court found unacceptable a Florida felony-murder rule that permitted persons who participate in crimes that result in the loss of human lives but who did not themselves commit a homicide offense. (Earl Enmund remained in a car while Sampson and Jeanette Armstrong approached a farmhouse with the apparent plan of committing a robbery. One or both of the Armstrongs then killed an 86-year-old man and his 74-year-old wife. Under Florida's felony-murder rule, which is found in the criminal law of a large number of jurisdictions, Enmund's involvement in the felony offense of armed robbery was sufficient to support a charge of first degree murder even though Enmund did not himself plan or become actively involved in the homicide offense.)

The abolitionists' position today, of course, is characterized by little more than despair and desperation. The victories won in such major cases as *Woolson, Roberts, Coker, Lockett,* and *Enmund* are, of course, significant. On the other hand, the number of persons now awaiting execution has reached a historic high, the actual number of executions has risen dramatically in the past few years, and there is growing evidence that the Supreme Court would like to limit the duration of appellate challenges to death sentences (e.g., *Barefoot v. Estelle,* 103 S.Ct. 3383, 1983; *Barclay v. Florida*, 103 S.Ct. 3418, 1983; and *Pulley v. Harris*, 104 S.Ct. 871, 1984). Over and above all of this is the fear that a combination of the conservative drift of the U.S. Supreme Court and the growing likelihood that President Reagan will be able to "stack" the court with one or more new justices will further undermine their position.

Evaluating the Uses and Abuses of the Death Penalty

Our quick trip through the recent history of capital punishment in the United States reveals both "good news and bad news" regardless of the position you might wish to adopt concerning this most extreme sentence. Certainly the number of people who can be defined as eligible for execution has narrowed considerably over the past five or ten years. Certainly the appellate courts remain committed to guaranteeing that the constitutional rights of defendants in capital cases be protected more jealously than they are in other contexts. At the same time, however, it is clear that all of these good intentions have not eliminated arbitrariness and discrimination. Either, on the one hand, receiving a sentence of death is very much like being struck by lightning or, on the other hand, it is too closely related to such factors as economic status, quality of defense counsel, prosecutorial preferences, sex, race, age, and a variety of victim-related variables.

Why, then, are so many of us so persuaded that the "life for a life" formula should continue to be applied within a cultural context that places so high a premium on the value of human life? Why is it, for example, that so many who are so committed to the "right to life" principle when they consider such morally and legally difficult issues as abortion and euthanasia are also so strongly supportive of the death penalty? (And I am not ignoring the paradox of many who strongly oppose the death penalty being so strongly in favor of especially permissive abortion and "right to die" statutes.) Is it possible that a large number of us are punitive, authoritarian, racist, or without empathy for those most disadvantaged portions of our population?

I and many others have raised this question repeatedly in our research (e.g., Thomas and Foster, 1975; Thomas and Cage, 1976; Thomas et al., 1977; Thomas, 1977; Vidmar and Miller, 1980). My own judgment is that such "negative explanations" as racism account for no more than a fraction of positive public, legislative, and judicial sentiment. More complete explanations, I think, may be found in two broad sets of variables. One of these has to do with perceptions of our criminal justice system which depict it as being, at least on balance, fair, reasonable, and correct as it goes about the business of determining who does and does not deserve especially harsh sentences. When, for example, we encounter information about death penalty cases being considered and then reconsidered by our courts over a period of multiple years, we tend to believe that any possibility of improper decisions would necessarily be detected and corrected.

Generally speaking, I agree with a portion of this viewpoint. Reasonable people surely differ regarding the holdings of appellate courts when they review cases involving death row inmates. Most, however, understand and appreciate the careful scrutiny these cases receive. However, much of the problem lies not in the relatively small number of cases involving offenders who received the death penalty but in the thousands of cases where prosecutors chose not to seek or juries and judges chose not to impose death sentences. There should be—but there is not now—a meaningful way of separating these two groups of offenders. Furthermore, too many of us are inclined to think of the judicial process as one that is self-correcting. The evidence suggests that it is not. Two of my friends—Hugo Adam Bedau, a philosopher affiliated with Tufts University, and Michael L. Radelet, a criminologist at the University of Florida—are now completing a comprehensive research project that demonstrates this fact quite emphatically. Their preliminary and as-yet-unpublished work documents some 350 cases in which defendants were convicted of capital crimes—including 100 in which death sentences were imposed and a dozen or so that resulted in executions—but who were later shown to be innocent persons.

The second major source of support for the death penalty is closely linked to the belief that executions deter crime. Always on the list of rationales advanced by those favoring capital punishment but never a position supported by any reliable statistical evidence despite decades of fairly careful research, this position found something of a new foundation in a widely publicized paper published by Erlich in 1975. In that statistically complex but conceptually sterile effort, Erlich argued that each execution prevented approximately eight homicides. I do not recall ever having seen any single piece of research having been so totally torn apart by so large a number of sophisticated critics (e.g., Baldus and Cole, 1975; Bowers and Pierce, 1975). My purpose, however, is not to further brutalize Erlich. Instead, I merely seek to point out two flatly contradictory conclusions. One is the public—and sometimes also the legislative and judicial—conclusion that the death penalty serves a deterrent purpose. The other, based on much research evidence, is that no acceptable scientific evidence points to a deterrent effect of executions (for a brief review, see Endres, 1985: 66-87, but for specific studies see Zeisel, 1976; Archer et al., 1983; Bailey, 1983; Baldus et al., 1983; Forst, 1983).

So where do we stand? We have a set of legal decisions that define the death penalty as constitutional under at least some circumstances for some categories of offenders. We have 37 states with death penalty statutes. We have 1540 persons awaiting executions in 32 states. A significant fraction of those persons will almost certainly be added to the more than 14,000 executions that have taken place in our legal history. We have a population within which perhaps three-quarters of all citizens are willing to support capital punishment. Ironically, however, our willingness to rely on so extreme a punishment seems to be closely tied to our faith in the fairness, the accuracy, and the future benefits we gain by the operation of our system of justice when the very best of the available evidence strongly suggests frequent inequity, a significant probability of error, and little or no prospect of tangible benefits.

SUMMARY AND CONCLUSIONS

A considerable amount of territory has been covered in this concluding chapter. While an apology must be extended for what the chapter could not provide by way of detail, it is hoped that this swift overview of the outer limits of penology has served some useful purposes. Indeed, in some ways the consideration of imprisonment and of the death penalty share something important in common. With regard to our use of imprisonment, it was shown that prisons fall within that category of rather specialized "people-processing" organizations that we have tried to design in our quest for ways of transforming human "raw material" into an acceptable "final product." Many of our efforts have been motivated by a laudatory commitment to making punishment something more than an end in and of itself by a sincere desire to do something that would simultaneously protect the larger society and transform offenders. But the very nature of the prison as an organization and the characteristics of the inmate society to which that organization contributes make efforts aimed at ill-defined goals of change all but impossible to achieve. Even if some temporary benefits were to be realized, most of what we now suggests that the problems associated with efforts of offenders to reintegrate themselves into the larger society upon their release from prison often undermine any benefits that prison might have achieved. Ignorant of how poor prisons are in achieving significantly more than the custodial goals to which they allocate the bulk of their resources, but also lacking any clearly defined alternative to our reliance on prisons, we now have a greater number of offenders—both in absolute and per capita terms—in prison than at any earlier point in penological history.

Many differences exist between our willingness to confine hundreds of thousands of offenders in prisons and our far less common willingness to impose sentences of death. Capital punishment in the United States has never been a sanction on which we have relied regularly, routinely, or for offenders who were not believed to have committed what were perceived to be especially serious crimes. Yet the persistent support for the death penalty is in many ways not so unlike the willingness to impose prison sentences. Large numbers of us see death sentences not only as a way of doing justice but also as a way of achieving such benefits as deterrence and incapacitation. Furthermore, especially when those viewed as eligible for death sentences have serious prior records of criminal involvement, we seem unable to imagine an acceptable alternative to so irrevocable a punishment. Contrary to the best available evidence regarding the utility of the death penalty, multiple defects in the methods by means of which sentences of death are imposed, and evidence about the real possibilities of errors, our beliefs and faith remain unshaken.

Thinking of our use of prisons and our continued willingness to rely on capital punishment is, I suspect, as appropriate a way as any to end this discussion of penology or, if you prefer, corrections in America. In this chapter as throughout this volume, it may seem unfortunate or even inappropriate that so many questions have been raised to which so few crisp, clean answers have been provided. That, however, is where the field of penology happens to be today. Criminologists have learned a good deal about what previous generations have tried to do with those who, for whatever good or bad reason, violated the provisions of criminal law. They have learned quite a lot about the illogic of many positions that have been taken regarding punishment as well as the ineffectiveness and unfairness that has attached to these positions. They can even make some reasonably good predictions of what consequences will follow from choices to adopt one strategy versus another.

Nevertheless, when all is said and done, it will not be the criminologists who will shape the future course of reactions to offenders. Many of the issues simply do not raise clear concerns of the type for which behavioral scientists can provide reasonable answers. The issues are moral and ethical and legal and political. To leave such matters to the "experts" would be, I think, to ask far more of those people than they have to offer. The power to punish is a power vested exclusively in the state. The power of the state is presumably no more or less than what is granted to it by its citizens. When any one of us confronts punishment, therefore, the nature, forms, and goals of that punishment are items for which we are individually as well as collectively responsible. Unfortunately, the record of history suggests that the job we have done falls somewhere in the dubious range that begins with brutality and ends with impotence. One is led to suspect that a brighter future will come in only one of two forms: a better class of offenders or a better informed, more thoughtful, and more responsible citizenry. Those who await that brighter future would be well advised not to hold their breath until either form of change materializes.

DISCUSSION QUESTIONS

Assume that you had no option available other than writing a death penalty statute that would immediately be enacted into law in your state. For what type(s) of offenses and for what type(s) of offenders would your statute permit or require the imposition of sentences of death? Justify your selection(s).

Assume that you have just been chosen to be the new warden of a major maximum security penitentiary. Are there steps that you would take to increase the likelihood that existing or new rehabilitative programs would be more effective? If so, why do you feel that such steps would work? If you see no such steps that could be taken, explain the reasons for your position.

CASES

REFERENCES

Akers, Ronald L., (1977) "Prisonization in five countries: type of prison and inmate characteristics." Criminology 14: 410-422.

———Norman S. Hayner, and Werner Grunginger (1974) "Homosexual and drug behavior in prison: a test of the functional and importation models of the inmate system." Social Problems 21: 410-422.

Alpert, Geoffrey P. (1980) Legal Rights of Prisoners. Beverly Hills, CA: Sage.

Alschuler, Albert W. (1978) "Sentencing reform and prosecutorial power: a critique of recent proposals for 'fixed' and 'presumptive' sentencing," pp. 59-88 in Determinate Sentencing: Reform or Regression. Washington, DC: U.S. Department of Justice.

American Friends Service Committee (1971) Sruggle for Justice. New York: Hill & Wang.

Archer, Dane, Rosemary Gartner, and Marc Beittel (1983) "Homicide and the death penalty: a cross-national test of a deterrence hypothesis." Journal of Criminal Law and Criminology 74: 991-1013.

Bailey, Walter C. (1966) "Correctional outcome: an evaluation of 100 reports." Journal of Criminal Law, Criminology, and Police Science 57: 153-160.

Bailey, William C. (1983) "Disaggregation in deterrence and death penalty research: the case of murder in Chicago." Journal of Criminal Law and Criminology 74: 827-859.

Baldus, David C. and James W. Cole (1975) "A comparison of the work of Thorsten Sellin and Isaac Ehrlich on the deterrent effect of capital punishment." Yale Law Review 85: 170-186.

Baldus, David C., Charles Pulaski, and George Woodworth (1983) "Comparative review of death sentences: an empirical study of the Georgia experience." Journal of Criminal Law and Criminology 74: 661-751.

Barlow, Hugh D. (1984) Introduction to Criminology. Boston: Little, Brown.

Barnes, Harry E. (1968) The Evolution of Penology in Pennsylvania. Montclair, NJ: Patterson-Smith. (Originally published 1927)

Beccaria, Cesare (1963) On Crimes and Punishment. Indianapolis: Bobbs-Merrill. (Originally published 1764; H. Paolucci, trans.)

Bedau, Hugo A. (1984) "Classification-based sentencing: some conceptual and ethical problems." New England Journal on Criminal and Civil Confinement 10: 1-26.

———(1983) "Capital punishment," pp. 133-143 in The Encyclopedia of Crime and Justice, Vol. 1. New York: Free Press.

———(1978) "Retribution and the theory of punishment." Journal of Philosophy 75: 601-620.

———(1977) The Courts, the Constitution, and Capital Punishment. Lexington, MA: D. C. Heath.

Bentele, Ursula (1985) "The death penalty in Georgia: still arbitrary." Washington University Law Quarterly 62: 573-615.

Bentham, Jeremy (1975) "The utilitarian theory of punishment," pp. 25-31 in J. Feinberg and H. Gross (eds.) Punishment. Belmont, CA: Dickenson.

Berk, Bernard B. (1966) "Organizational goals and inmate organization." American Journal of Sociology 71: 522-534.

Berman, Harold J. (1983) Law and Revolution: The Formation of the Western Legal Tradition. Cambridge, MA: Harvard University Press.

Black, Charles L., Jr. (1982) Capital Punishment: The Inevitability of Caprice and Mistake. New York: W. W. Norton.

Black, Donald (1976) The Behavior of Law. New York: Academic Press.

———(1970) "The production of crime rates." American Sociological Review 35: 733-748.

Blau, Peter M. and W. Richard Scott (1962) Formal Organizations: A Comparative Approach: San Francisco: Chandler.

Blumstein, Alfred, Jacqueline Cohen, and Daniel Nagin [eds.] (1978) Deterrence and Incapacitation: Estimating the Effects of Criminal Sanctions on Crime Rates. Washington, DC: National Academy of Sciences.

Bowers, William J. (1983) "The pervasiveness of arbitrariness and discrimination under post-Furman capital statutes." Journal of Criminal Law and Criminology 74: 1067-1100.

———— and Glenn L. Pierce (1980) "Arbitrariness and discrimination under post-*Furman* statutes." Crime and Delinquency 26: 563-635.

Bowker, Lee H. (1977) Prisoner Subcultures. Lexington, MA: D. C. Heath.

Brim, Orville G., Jr. and Stanton Wheeler (1966) Socialization after Childhood: Two Essays. New York: John Wiley.

Bronstein, Alvin J. (1984) "Criminal justice: prisons and penology," pp. 221-236 in N. Dorsen (ed.) Our Endangered Rights: The ACLU Report on Civil Liberties Today. New York: Pantheon.

Brosi, Kathleen B. (1979) A Cross-City Comparison of Felony Case Processing. Washington, DC: U.S. Department of Justice.

Brown, Edward J., Timothy J. Flanagan, and Maureen McLeod [eds.] (1984) Sourcebook of Criminal Justice Statistics, 1983. Washington, DC: Government Printing Office.

Bureau of Justice Statistics (1985a) Prisoners in 1984. Washington, DC: U.S. Department of Justice.

————(1985b) Examining Recidivism. Washington, DC: U.S. Department of Justice.

————(1984a) Households Touched by Crime, 1983. Washington, DC: U.S. Department of Justice.

————(1984b) Criminal Victimization in the United States, 1982. Washington, DC: U.S. Department of Justice.

————(1984c) Capital Punishment, 1982. Washington, DC: U.S. Department of Justice.

————(1984d) The Prevalence of Guilty Pleas. Washington, DC: U.S. Department of Justice.

————(1984e) The 1983 Jail Census. Washington, DC: U.S. Department of Justice.

————(1984f) Probation and Parole, 1983. Washington, DC: U.S. Department of Justice.

————(1983) Report to the Nation on Crime and Justice. Washington, DC: U.S. Department of Justice.

————(1982) Prisons and Prisoners. Washington, DC: U.S. Department of Justice.

————(1981) Expenditure and Employment Data for the Criminal Justice System, 1978. Washington, DC: U.S. Department of Justice.

Carroll, Leo (1974) Hacks, Blacks, and Cons: Race Relations in a Maximum Security Prison. Lexington, MA: D. C. Heath.

———— and Margaret E. Mondrick (1976) "Racial bias in the decision to grant parole." Law and Society Review 11: 93-107.

Carter, Robert M. and Leslie T. Wilkins [eds.] (1970) Probation and Parole: Selected Readings. New York: John Wiley.

Cavender, Gray (1982) Parole: A Critical Analysis. Port Washington, NY: Kennikat Press.

Chambliss, W. and Robert Seidman (1982) Law, Order, and Power. Reading, MA: Addison-Wesley.

Clemmer, Donald (1958) The Prison Community. New York: Holt, Rinehart & Winston. (Originally published 1940)

Cloward, Richard A. (1960) "Social control in the prison," pp. 20-48 in Richard A. Cloward et al. (eds.) Theoretical Studies in the Social Organization of the Prison. New York: Social Science Research Council.

Conklin, John E. (1981) Criminology. New York: Macmillan.

Conrad, Peter and Joseph W. Schneider (1980) Deviance and Medicalization: From Badness to Sickness. St. Louis: C. V. Mosby.

Cressey, Donald R. (1982) "Foreword," pp. xi-xxiii in F. Cullen and K. Gilbert, Reaffirming Rehabilitation. Cincinnati: Anderson.

Cullen, Francis T. and Karen E. Gilbert (1982) Reaffirming Rehabilitation. Cincinnati: Anderson.

Diana, Lewis (1960) "What is probation?" Journal of Criminal Law, Criminology and Police Science 51: 189-204.

Duster, Troy (1970) The Legislation of Morality: Law, Drugs, and Moral Judgment. New York: Free Press.

Ehrlich, Isaac (1975) "The deterrent effect of capital punishment: a question of life and death." American Economic Review 65: 397-417.

Eisenstein, J. and H. Jacobs (1977) Felony Justice. Boston: Little, Brown.

Endres, Michael E. (1985) The Morality of Capital Punishment: Equal Justice Under the Law? Mystic, CT: Twenty-Third.

Eriksson, Torsten (1976) The Reformers. New York: Elsevier.

Etzioni, Amitai (1975) A Comparative Analysis of Complex Organizations. New York: Free Press.

————— (1964) Modern Organizations. Englewood Cliffs, NJ: Prentice-Hall.

Ezorksky, Gertrude [ed.] (1972) Philosophical Perspectives on Punishment. Albany: State University of New York Press.

Farr, Kathryn Ann (1984) "Administration and justice: maintaining balance through an institutionalized plea negotiation process." Criminology 22: 291-319.

Feinbert, Joel and Hyman Gross [eds.] (1975) Punishment: Selected Readings. Belmont, CA: Dickenson.

Fletcher, George P. (1978) Rethinking Criminal Law. Boston: Little, Brown.

Fogel, David (1975) We Are the Living Proof: The Justice Model for Corrections. Cincinnati: Anderson.

————— and Joe Hudson [eds.] (1981) Justice as Fairness: Perspectives on the Justice Model. Cincinnati: Anderson.

Forst, Brian (1983) "Capital punishment and deterrence: conflicting evidence?" Journal of Criminal Law and Criminology 74: 927-942.

Fox, Vernon (1985) Introduction to Criminology. Englewood Cliffs, NJ: Prentice-Hall.

Gaes, Gerald G. (1985) "The effects of overcrowding in prison," pp. 95-146 in M. Tonry and N. Morris (eds.) Crime and Justice, Vol. 6. Chicago: University of Chicago Press.

Garabedian, Peter G. (1963) "Social roles and processes of socialization in the prison community." Social Problems 11: 140-151.

Gardner, Thomas J. and Victor Manian (1980) Criminal Law: Principles, Cases, and Readings. St. Paul, MN: West.

Garfinkel, Harold (1956) "Conditions of successful degradation ceremonies." American Journal of Sociology 61: 420-434.

Gerber, Rudolph J. and Patrick D. McAnany [eds.] (1972) Contemporary Punishment: Views, Explanations, and Justifications. Notre Dame, IN: University of Notre Dame Press.

Giallombardo, Rose (1966) Society of Women: A Study of a Woman's Prison. New York: John Wiley.

Gibbs, Jack P. (1980) "The death penalty, retribution, and penal policy." Journal of Criminal Law and Criminology 69: 291-299.

Glaser, Daniel (1964) The Effectiveness of a Prison and Parole System. Indianapolise: Bobbs-Merrill.

Goebel, Julius, Jr. (1976) Felony and Misdemeanor: A Study in the History of Criminal Law. Philadelphia: University of Pennsylvania Press.

Goffman, Erving (1981a) Asylums: Essays on the Social Situation of Mental Patients and Other Inmates: New York: Anchor Books.

—————(1981b) "On the characteristics of toal institutions: the inmate world," pp. 15-67 in D. Cressey (ed.) The Prison: Studies in Institutional Organization and Change. New York: Holt, Rinehart & Winston.

—————(1961) The Asylum. Baltimore: Penguin Books.

Goodstein, Lynne (1979) "Inmate adjustments to prison and the transition to community life." Journal of Research in Crime and Delinquency 16: 246-272.

————— and Doris L. MacKenzie (1984) "Racial differences in adjustment patterns of prison inmates: prisonization, conflict, stress, and control," in D. E. Georges-Abeyie (ed.) Blacks, Crime and Justice. New York: Clark Boardman.

Greenberg, David F. and Drew Humphries (1980) "The cooptation of fixed sentence reform." Crime and Delinquency 26: 206-225.

Gross, Hyman and Andrew von Hirsch [eds.] (1981) Sentencing. New York: Oxford University Press.

Grusky, Oscar (1959) "Organizational goals and the behavior of inmate leaders." American Journal of Sociology 65: 59-67.

Hart, H.L.A. (1968) Punishment and Responsibility: Essays in the Philosophy of Law. London: Oxford University Press.

Heffernan, Esther (1972) Making it in Prison: The Square, the Cool, and the Life. New York: John Wiley.

Hepburn, John R. (1977) "Social control and the legal order: legitimated repression in a capitalist state." Contemporary Crises 1: 77-90.

Heumann, M. (1975) "A note on plea bargaining and case pressure." Law and Society Review 9: 515-528.

Honderich, Ted (1971) Punishment: Its Supposed Justification. Baltimore: Penguin Books.

Irwin, John (1980) Prisons in Turmoil. Boston: Little, Brown.

———(1970) The Felon. Englewood Cliffs, NJ: Prentice-Hall.

——— and Donald R. Cressey (1962) "Thieves, convicts, and the inmate culture." Social Problems 10: 142-155.

Jacobs, James B. (1979) "Race relations and the prisoner subculture," pp. 1-28 in N. Morris and M. Tonry (eds.) Crime and Justice, Vol. 1. Chicago: University of Chicago Press.

———(1977) Stateville: The Penitentiary in Mass Society. Chicago: University of Chicago Press.

Jenkins, Philip (1984) Crime and Justice: Issues and Ideas. Monterey, CA: Brooks/Cole.

Jensen, Gary F. (1977) "Age and rule-breaking in prison: a test of sociological interpretations." Criminology 14: 565-570.

Johns, C.H.W. [trans.] (1903) The Oldest Code of Laws in the World: The Code of Laws Promulgated by Hammurabi, King of Babylon, B.C. 2285-2242. Edinburgh: T. & T. Clark.

Karpman, Benjamin (1973) "Criminal psychodynamics: a platform," pp. 118-132 in Jeffrie G. Murphy (ed.) Punishment and Rehabilitation. Belmont, CA: Wadsworth.

———(1956) "Criminal psychodynamics." Journal of Criminal Law, Criminology, and Police Science 47: 8-17.

Kassenbaum, Gene, David Ward, and Daniel Wilner (1971) Prison Treatment and Parole Survival: An Empirical Assessment. New York: John Wiley

Kaufman, Walter (1973) Without Guilt and Innocence: From Decidophobia to Autonomy. New York: Dell.

Kempin, Frederick G., Jr. (1973) Historical Introduction to Anglo-American Law. St. Paul, MN: West.

———(1963) Legal History: Law and Social Change. Engelwood Cliffs, NJ: Prentice-Hall.

Kerper, Hazel and Janeen Kerper (1974) Legal Rights of the Convicted. St. Paul, MN: West.

King, Thomas A. (1982) "An analysis of the jurisprudence of cruel and unusual punishment." Ph.D. dissertation, West Virginia University.

Kittrie, Nicholas N. and Elyce H. Zenoff (1981) Sanctions, Sentencing, and Corrections. Mineola, NY: Foundation Press.

Krisberg, Barry (1975) Crime and Privilege: Toward a New Criminology. Englewood Cliffs, NJ: Prentice-Hall.

——— and James Austin (1978) The Children of Ishmael: Critical Perspectives on Juvenile Justice. Palo Alto, CA: Mayfield.

Lerman, Paul (1975) Community Treatment and Social Control: A Critical Analysis of Juvenile Correctional Policy. Chicago: University of Chicago Press.

Lewis, W. David (1965) From Newgate to Dannemora: The Rise of the Penitentiary in New York, 1796-1848. Ithaca, NY: Cornell Univesity Press.

Lindesmith, Alfred R. (1965) The Addict and the Law. Bloomington: Indiana University Press.

Lipton, Douglas, Robert Martinson, and Judith Wilks (1975) The Effectiveness of Correctional Treatment: A Survey of Treatment Evaluation Studies: New York: Praeger.

Logan, Charles H. (1972) "Evaluation research in crime and delinquency: a reappraisal." Journal of Criminal Law, Criminology, and Police Science 63: 378-387.

Lombroso, Cesare (1968) Crime: Its Causes and Remedies. Montclair, NJ: Patterson-Smith. (Originally published 1912)

Lombroso-Ferrero, Gina (1972) Lombroso's Criminal Man. Monclair, NJ: Patterson-Smith. (Originally published 1911)

Maestro, Marcello (1973) Cesare Beccaria and the Origins of Penal Reform. Philadelphia: Temple University Press.

McCorkle, Lloyd W. and Richard Korn (1954) "Resocialization within walls." The Annals 293: 89-103.

McKelvey, Blake (1976) American Prisons: A History of Good Intentions. Montclair, NJ: Patterson-Smith.

Meltsner, Michael (1973) Cruel and Unusual: The Supreme Court and Capital Punishment. New York: Random House.

Menninger, Karl (1968) The Crime of Punishment. New York: Viking.

Michalowski, Raymond J. (1985) Order, Law, and Crime: An Introduction to Criminology. New York: Random House.

Mitford, Jessica (1974) Kind and Usual Punishment. New York: Vintage.

Moczydlowski, Pawel (1983) "Types of penal institution, economic organization, and inmate social structure: some Polish examples." International Journal of the Sociology of Law 11: 305-315.

Morris, Norval (1982) Madness and the Law. Chicago: University of Chicago Press.

——(1974) The Future of Imprisonment. Chicago: University of Chicago Press.

—— and Marc Miller (1985) "Predictions of dangerousness," pp. 1-50 in M. Tonry and N. Morris (eds.) Crime and Justice, Vol. 6. Chicago: University of Chicago Press.

Murphy, Jeffrie G. [ed.] (1973) Punishment and Rehabilitation. Belmont, CA: Wadsworth.

Nettler, Gwynn (1984) Explaining Crime. New York: McGraw-Hill.

Office of Juvenile Justice and Delinquency Prevention (1983) "Children in custody: advance report on the 1982 census of public juvenile facilities." Washington, DC: U.S. Department of Justice.

Ohlin, Lloyd E. (1956) Sociology and the Field of Corrections. New York: Russell Sage Foundation.

Packer, Herbert L. (1968) Limits of the Criminal Sanction. Stanford, CA: Stanford University Press.

Palmer, John W. (1977) Constitutional Rights of Prisoners. Cincinnati: Anderson.

Paternoster, Raymond (1984) "Prosecutorial discretion in requesting the death penalty: a case of victim-based racial discrimination." Law and Society Review 18: 437-460.

——(1983) "Race of victim and location of crime: the decision to seek the death penalty in South Carolina." Journal of Criminal Law and Criminology 74: 754-785.

Perkins, Rollin M. and Ronald N. Boyce (1982) Criminal Law. Mineola, NY: The Foundation Press.

Petersilia, Joan (1983) Racial Disparities in the Criminal Justice System. Santa Monica, CA: Rand.

Pincoffs, Edmund L. (1966) The Rationale of Legal Punishment. New York: Humanities Press.

Poole, Eric D., Robert M. Regoli, and Charles W. Thomas (1980) "The measurement of inmate social roles: an assessment." Journal of Criminal Law and Criminology 71: 317-324.

Pope, Carl E. (1975) Sentencing of California Felony Offenders. Washington, DC: U.S. Department of Justice.

Post, C. Gordon (1963) An Introduction to the Law. Englewood Cliffs, NJ: Prentice-Hall.

Quinney, Richard (1979) Criminology. Boston: Little, Brown.

Radelet, Michael L. (1981) "Racial characteristics and the imposition of the death penalty." American Sociological Review 46: 918-927.

—— and Glenn L. Pierce (1985) "Race and prosecutorial discretion in homicide cases." Law and Society Review, forthcoming.

Radelet, Michael L. and Margaret Vandiver (1983) "The Florida Supreme Court and death penalty appeals." Journal of Criminal Law and Criminology 74: 913-926.

Rawls, John (1971) A Theory of Justice. Cambridge, MA: Harvard University Press.

——(1956) "Two concepts of rules." Philosophical Review 64: 3-32.

Riedel, Marc (1976) "Death row 1975: A study of offenders sentenced under post-*Furman* statutes." Temple Law Quarterly 49: 261-286.

—— and Terence P. Thornberry (1978) "The effectiveness of correctional programs: an assessment of the field," pp. 318-432 in Barry Krisberg and James Austin (eds.) The Children of Ishmael. Palo Alto, CA: Mayfield.

Rossett, Arthur and Donald R. Cressey (1976) Justice by Consent: Plea Bargains in the American Courthouse. Philadelphia: J. B. Lippincott.

Rothman, David J. (1971) The Discovery of the Asylum: Social Order and Disorder in the New Republic. Boston: Little, Brown.

Rusche, Georg and Kircheimer (1939) Punishment and Social Structure. New York: Columbia University Press.

Schrag, Clarence G. (1961) "Some foundations for a theory of correction," pp. 309-357 in D. Cressey (ed.) The Prison: Studies in Institutional Organization and Change. New York: Holt, Rinehart & Winston.

——(1944) "Social types in a prison community." M.A. thesis, University of Washington.

Schwartz, Barry (1971) "Pre-institutional vs. situational influence in a correctional community." Journal of Criminal Law, Criminology, and Police Science 62: 530-545.

Schwartz, Richard D. and Jerome H. Skolnick (1962) "Two studies of legal stigma." Social Problems 10: 133-142.

Smith, Joan and William Fried (1974) The Uses of The American Prison: Political Theory and Penal Practice. Lexington, MA: D. C. Heath.

Stanley, David T. (1981) "The parole board hearing," pp. 231-243 in R. Culbertson and M. Tezak (eds.) Order Under Law: Readings in Criminal Justice. Prospect Heights, IL: Waveland Press.

Street, David, Robert Vinter, and Charles Perrow (1966) Organization for Treatment. New York: Free Press.

Streib, Victor L. (1983) "Death penalty for children: the American experience with capital punishment for crimes committed while under age eighteen." Oklahoma Law Review 36: 613-641.

Sutton, L. Paul (1978) Federal Sentencing Patterns: A Study of Geographical Variations. Washington, DC: U.S. Department of Justice.

Sykes, Gresham M. (1966) The Society of Captives. New York: Atheneum.

———(1960) "The inmate social system," pp. 5-19 in R. Cloward et al. (eds.) Theoretical Studies in the Social Organization of the Prison. New York: Social Science Research Council.

Szasz, Thomas S. (1970) Ideology and Insanity: Essays on the Psychiatric Dehumanization of Man. Garden City, NY: Doubleday.

Thomas, Charles W. (1977) "Prisonization and its consequences: an examination of socialization in a coercive setting." Sociological Focus 10: 53-68.

———(1975) "Prisonization of resocialization: a study of external factors associated with the impact of imprisonment." Journal of Research in Crime and Delinquency 10: 13-21.

———(1970) "Toward a more inclusive model of the inmate contraculture." Criminology 8: 251-262.

——— and Shay Bilchik (1985) "Prosecuting juveniles in criminal courts: a legal and an empirical analysis." Journal of Criminal Law and Criminology 76.

Thomas, Charles W. and Donna M. Bishop (1984) "The impact of legal sanctions on delinquency: an assessment of the utility of labeling and deterrence theories." Journal of Criminal Law and Criminology 75: 1222-1245.

Thomas, Charles W. and Matthew J. Bronick (1984) "The quality of doctoral programs in deviance, criminology, and criminal justice: an empirical assessment." Journal of Criminal Justice 12: 21-38.

Thomas, Charles W. and Robin J. Cage (1977) "Correlates of prison drug use." Criminology 15: 193-210.

———(1976) "Correlates of public attitudes toward legal sanctions." International Journal of Criminology and Penology 4: 239-255.

——— and Samuel C. Foster (1977) "Public opinion on criminal law and legal sanctions." Journal of Criminal Law and Criminology 67: 110-116.

Thomas, Charles W. and W. Anthony Fitch (1977) "The exercise of discretionary-making by the police." North Dakota Law Review 54: 61-95.

Thomas, Charles W. and Samuel C. Foster (1975) "A sociological perspective on public support for the death penalty." American Journal of Orthopsychiatry 45: 641-657.

———(1973) "The importation model perspective on inmate social role adaptations." Sociological Quarterly 14: 226-234.

———(1972) "Prisonization in the inmate contraculture." Social Problems 20: 229-239.

Thomas, Charles W. and John R. Hepburn (1983) Crime, Criminal Law, and Criminology. Dubuque, IA: Wiliam C. Brown.

Thomas, Charles W. and R. Gregg Howard (1977) "Public attitudes toward capital punishment: a comparative analysis." Journal of Behavioral Economics 6: 189-216.

Thomas, Charles W. and David M. Petersen (1977) Prison Organization and Inmate Subcultures. Indianapolis: Bobbs-Merrill.

Thomas, Charles W. and Eric D. Poole (1975) "The consequences of incompatible goal structures in correctional settings." International Journal of Criminology and Penology 3: 37-42.

Toch, Hans (1977) Living in Prison: The Ecology of Survival. New York: Free Press.

Twentieth Century Fund Task Force on Criminal Sentencing (1976) Fair and Certain Punishment. New York: McGraw-Hill.

Ullman, Walter (1975) Law and Politics in the Middle Ages: An Introduction to the Sources of Medieval Political Ideas. Ithaca, NY: Cornell University Press.

U.S. Department of Justice (1982) Crime in the United States. Washington, DC: Government Printing Office.

————(1979) Profile of State Prison Inmates: Sociodemographic Findings from the 1974 Survey of Inmates in State Correctional Facilities. Washington, DC: Government Printing Office.

van den Haag, Ernest (1975) Punishing Criminals: Concerning a Very Old and Painful Question. New York: Basic Books.

Vidmar, Neil and Dale T. Miller (1980) "Social psychological processes underlying attitudes toward legal punishment. Law and Society Review 14: 565-602.

Vold, George B. and Thomas J. Bernard (1979) Theoretical Criminology. New York: Oxford University Press.

von Hirsch, Andrew (1976) Doing Justice. New York: Hill & Wang.

Wellford, Charles (1967) "Factors associated with adoption of the inmate code: a study of normative socialization." Journal of Criminal Law, Criminology, and Police Science 58: 197-203.

Wilkins, Leslie (1969) Evaluation of Penal Methods. New York: John Wiley.

Wolfgang, Marvin E. and Marc Riedel (1973) "Race, judicial discretion, and the death penalty." The Annals 407: 119-133.

Zatz, Marjorie, S. (1985) "Pleas, priors and prison: racial/ethnic differences in sentencing." Social Science Research 14: 169-193.

————(1984) "Race, ethnicity, and determinate sentencing." Criminology 22: 147-171.

———— and John Hagan (1985) "Crime, time, and punishment: an exploration of selection bias in sentencing research." Journal of Quantitative Criminology 1: 103-126.

Zeisel, Hans (1981) "The disposition of felony arrests." American Bar Foundation Research Journal 407-462.

————(1976) "The deterrent effect of the death penalty: facts versus faith," pp. 317-343 in P. B. Kurland (ed.) The Supreme Court Review. Chicago: University of Chicago Press.

INDEX

ABOUT THE AUTHOR

Charles W. Thomas is currently a Professor of Criminology and Director of the Center for Studies in Criminology and Law at the University of Florida. His primary research interests are in the areas of corrections, the sociology of law, and juvenile law. His previous work has appeared in such publications as the *Journal of Criminal Law and Criminology, Social Problems, Criminal Law Journal Review, The Sociological Quarterly*, and a variety of other research journals and law reviews. He also is the author of several book-length works such as *Crime, Criminal Law, and Criminology; Prison Organization and Inmate Subcultures;* and *Criminal Law: Understanding Basic Principles.*